SIXTY-FOUR YEARS TO MAKE A NEGRO !

(*READ WILLIE LYNCH'S SPEECH TO THE SLAVE-OWNERS OF 1712!*)

Theme of the Book!

Learn how the Blackwoman was forced to teach and train her off-springs how to be slaves in order to survive. This slave mentality must be removed from the Unconscious Mind of the Blackman and Woman of America to be Free.

SIXTY- FOUR YEARS TO MAKE A NEGRO !

(*WILLIE LYNCH SPEECH TO THE AMERICAN SLAVE-OWNERS OF 1712!*)

ALFRED ALI

Published by:
Alfred Ali Literary Works
P.O. Box 27206
Detroit, Mi. 48227

FIRST EDITION

Copyright 1995 by Alfred Ali

Published by:
AA Literary works, Inc.
PO. Box 27206
Detroit, Mi. 48227

Manufactured in the United States of America
ISBN 0-9636025-3-5
Library of Congress catalog No: 94-073228

Distributor:
Merle Book Distributor. Inc.
27222 Plymouth Rd
Detroit, Mi. 48239
1-800-233-9380

DEDICATION

This book is dedicated to my Wife and Companion Martha Ali, also to my children James Alfred and Joanna. My mother Mrs. Louise Johnson and brothers James, Lawrence, Clauzell, Oscar and Cephus. To all who have helped me in this endeavor, and a special thanks to Firefighters Joseph Ampah and Jerry Sample for their computer skills, Orlando Gregory for his courage and friendship and Angela Story for her reference on slavery. Also, a special thanks to Commissioner Watkins for coming out of retirement.

TABLE OF CONTENTS

contents vii.

Contents viii.

Contents x.

PREFACE:

Man's Search for Heaven (Money, Drugs, and Power).

Genesis 2:22 and 24, and the rib, which the Lord God had taken from Man, made he a Woman, and brought her unto the Man. 24 Therefore a man shall leave his father and mother, and shall cleave unto his wife; and they shall be one flesh.

The purpose and intent of this book is to show that Man has been looking for heaven in all the wrong places. He has sought it in Alcohol, Drugs i.e. cocaine, opium, and Power of over men through slavery, and the abuse of women.He has searched the sky and proclaimed that he will see it after he dies. Due to his own ignorance, he has failed to realize that God has provided his heaven in the woman. She is his comfort in times of need, and provides peace to his Mind like nothing else in this world. She reproduces himself through the woman and without her life is not worth living. The problem is understanding the self-image of the Man and Woman.

A True Self-Image is the foundation upon which a nation builds its Culture, Religion, History, Names, Dietary Laws, Mannerism, and Economy. The self-image is a mental picture of Who You Think That You Are; As A Man Thinketh So Is He. The self-image determines our Beliefs and Behaviors and they are always consistent with our conception of ourselves. There are two self-images that must be discussed for clarity and that is the self-image of the Blackman and the Whiteman.

The home of the Blackman is in the fertile crescent along the Nile River, the Mediterranean and the warm climatic area now know as the Middle East or Africa. All of the world's Prophets and Religions have evolved out of this area such as Abraham, Issac, Jacob,Muhammad and Jesus. This land is also referred to as The Promise Land or The Holy Land, the Pyramids, Sphinx, Language, and Art all evolve out of the civilization of Ethiopia or Holy Land. Which was the first civilization on which other societies patterned their lifestyles.

So the Spiritual Image of the Blackman is that of a Righteous Man of society, His base is God and the scripture that comes from him is from holy men. These scriptures are known as the Books of the Bible, Torah, and Holy Quran. The original intent of the Bible was to be a guidance for God's people and it was written using the names of their homeland. However, the scripture was taken to Europe, the home of the Caucasians and Re-Written In Their Own Image!

The Caucasians showed all of the Prophets, Abraham, Moses, and Jesus looking like them, and God's People looking like them and called this new Religion Christianity. This created a New self-image for the Whiteman and made him appear to the world as a Divine People. THIS IS NOT TRUE! What is the true self-image of the Whiteman? The true self-image of the Whiteman (Spiritual-Image) was stated by Jesus in John 8: 39-44 They answered, and said unto him .

Abraham is our father. Jesus said unto them if you were Abraham's children , ye would do the works of Abraham. 40 But now ye seek to kill me, a man that hath told ye the truth, which I have heard of God, this did not Abraham. 41 Ye do the deeds of your father. Then said they to him, We are not born of fornication; We have one Father, even God. 42 Jesus said unto them if God were your Father, ye would love me; for I proceedeth forth and came from God; neither came I of myself, but he sent me. 43 Why do ye not understand my speech? Even because ye cannot hear my word. 44 Ye are of your father the devil, and the lusts of your father ye will do. He was a murderer from the beginning and abode not in the truth, because there is no truth in him. When he speaketh a lie, he speaketh of his own; for he is a liar, and the father of it.

The reason for showing the two self-images is that throughout the book you will see that he is constantly taking away from nations their rightful image of themselves, and claiming (stealing) their heritage as his own. It is being done in the Middle East with Israel (Whiteman) claiming the Holy Land for himself as his heritage. America was taken from the Indians. The African American was stolen from Africa and still can't get full citizenship because remember what Jesus said: The self-image is not of God. The Dutch has taken over South Africa from the Africans, the British control the Caribbean and it is a world-wide conspiracy of control.

The Spiritual self-image of the Blackman is of a Righteous Man, and the Spiritual Self-Image of the Whiteman is not of Truth, as state by Jesus John 8: 39-44. They were given 6,000 years to rule the earth, this will be repeated several times within the book for clarity. The first 2,000 years were spent in the caves and hills of Europe as a Divine chastisement for breaking God's Laws. The next 2,000 years were the building of civilization in Europe, Athens, Greece and the Roman Empire. The last 2,000 years begins with Jesus Christ , who identifies them as people who cannot be reformed unless they are physically, mentally, and spiritually Reborn in God. The aim and purpose of this book is to illustrate that the Blackman of scripture is the Prophets or Messengers of God that tries to reform Unrighteous people.

A True Slave is a person or nation that is capture mentally, and spiritually to another nation's ideas, culture, history, economics and religion. A Prophet is sent to these people to "Teach them to Do For Themselves" but he is normally rejected, and treated as an outcast or as a black sheep within that nation. It is not the job of a Prophet to destroy the people but only to deliver the message. God will destroy the people after the message has been delivered. After Lot came the Fire, After Noah came the flood, After Moses came the drowning of Pharaoh, After Jesus Rome self-destruct, After Muhammad came the Crusades, and after this Last Black Sheep, Who knows what the destruction will be ?

In this book the Black Sheep is sent from God to reform and deliver a message to a slavery-minded people and free them from the destructive behavior and life-style of their oppressor. If they do not accept the message then the oppressor , and the slaves that refuse the message will be destroyed. The True self-image of a Black Sheep is that of a Reformer; A man sent from God with a message to real slavery-minded people tied to another man's culture and way of life. The physical chains are the first part of slavery but real slavery takes place within the Mind of the individual that accepts another man as his master; instead of God. The premise of this book is that Blackman does not know that God dwells within himself and is a slave to his emotions and others of superior knowledge.

The spiritual principle that the Blackman is missing is Bible 1 Corinthian 3:16 Know ye not that ye are the temple of God, and that the Spirit of God dwells in you? The Blackman is a slave to illicit sexual behavior, money and what it will purchase, and his Mind iscontrolled by the ideas, and thoughts of the Whiteman's society. The slave (Blackman) grieves for the money or wealth that the Rich Man (Whiteman) has and this mental and spiritual grief is the cause of his hell on earth. Until the Blackman learns to build his own tree of wealth (nation) he will always be a mental and spiritual slave to the Whiteman. Spiritually, the Blackman is a slave to Scripture because he thinks that White People are Divine and the Chosen People of God;

The premise of this book is that Money is the root cause of a person or nation that is enslaved. Slavery is a business mentally, culturally, morally, historically, and politically. The Blackman of America is a perfect example of Money and slavery working together to build a country.

INTRODUCTION:

THE BLACK WOMAN TRUE IMAGE

Genesis 1-2 In the Beginning, God created the heaven and the earth. 2 And the Earth was without form, and void, darkness was upon the face of the deep . And the Spirit of God moved upon the face of the waters. God's Spirit was within the Blackness! A Divine state of Mind evolving out of pure darkness. A Mind of Righteousness and Goodness. All life evolves out of darkness into the light. Revelation 2:1 He that hath an ear, let him hear what the spirit saith unto the churches: To him that overcometh will I give to eat of the Tree of Life.

The Tree of Life is a Way of Life ordained by God that has within it the knowledge of Good and Evil, and all of the richness that God has provided for the righteous.

This teachings is about the Blackman and woman being raised from the dead mentally and spiritually. They do not know themselves Divinely and are being raised gradually into the knowledge of God, Devil, and Self. The Blackman and woman has an opportunity to show the world how God, through man and woman builds a civilization known as a Tree of Life. The Blackman and woman of America must be given a new Identity that will enable them to build a new self-concept based on God's infinite wisdom. The problem is mis-information or lies that are taught about the history of the blackman and the real nature of the human being.

xvii.

What is the purpose of Religion? The purpose of Religion in the life of human beings is to give the Mind a viewpoint to that will enable the person to see right from wrong, good from bad, or the two-sides of life; thus the individual is able to decide which Way of Life he or she wants to live. God is a Spirit, however, this spirit dwells within the human being, so God and the human are One. When the spirit is operating according to God's laws, rules, and behavior within the individual, then this person is considered Spiritual.

The Spirit is Creative. The Spirit creates within a process and not instantaneous. The Birth cycle is the best example of how the spirit works in a woman. The birth cycle of conception, gestation, and birth is a good indicator of a process. Most people think of God creating the world instantly like "Be and there it is!"However, the true meaning of this phrase is "Whatever God conceives in his Mind is instant because Time does not exist with God" but with humans, Time is needed to process the Idea or Thought into matter.

The true Image of A Woman is Creativity because she give birth or creates the human being within her womb. She is the Mother of Civilization. She is the first teacher. She is the foundation of the home, and the bridge that the children use to enter into society. Because of being stripped of the knowledge of herself in slavery in America, she has not being taught how to use her creative powers.

First, the right way of Thinking, second, the right way of dressing, third, the right relationship between husband and wife, which is covered in depth later on in this book. The Blackwoman is not able to gain new heights and growth because it is not expected of her. Spiritually speaking, the reason most black people have such a hard time coming together in unity is because they have not recognized the value of the Blackwoman.

God is making a new people in America, out of the Blackman and Woman, and to be resurrected means to rise in status through Divine Guidance. It can never be done through Affirmative Action or any other government program because of Racism and living with a Racist people. It must come through Divine Intervention Revelation 21:5 Behold, I make All Things New. God is removing from the Blackman and Woman that old Negro Way of Thinking and instilling within them A New Way of Thinking based on the Divine Revelation of his Word.

Those who Believe and Practice his Words will develop A New Mind (Way of Thinking) and this New Mind will enable them to build a New Community for themselves. They cannot build a community on the old knowledge of the Negroes . The Blackwoman will be made into a new woman. She will dress different, talk different, Act different and Think different. She will once again represent the Mother of Civilization in the new community of God. The foundation of this teachings is that Many are Called, but Few are chosen.

Introduction xx.

The few that are chosen to build the foundation for this nation or community of God will be recognized as the Children of God. This teachings will correct the conditions of a poverty-mentality, slavery consciousness, and a lack of the knowledge of self. The spiritual awakening that is taking place all over the world is being brought about by the power of Almighty God as taught in scripture (Bible and Holy Quran).

The Blackwoman must be placed back into the natural order of things as ordained byAllah (God), by re-teaching her real Identity. She must be taught the Divine Truth so she can decide of her own free-will to choose right from wrong. To being virtuous in all aspects of life. She must decide to serve God or the Devil. No one can serve two masters, for either You will hate one and Love the other because you cannot serve God and the Devil. The True Image of the Blackwoman is Fidelity, Kindness, Love, Chastity, Long-suffering, Righteousness, and the Mother of Civilization. The woman is the standard bearer by which a nation is respected in the world community. When the Image of the woman is perverted, distorted, and mis-represented in the world-community then that nation loses pride and is not respected as a civilized nation.

Any nation that has pride in it-self must hold its women high on a pedestal because they represents the nation's honor. As long as the Blackman of America has a low conception or opinion of his woman then he is not fit to rise as a nation.

xx.

However, this is all changing as the Blackman is re-educated into the knowledge of himself and the knowledge of the Blackwoman. This book is to designed to give knowledge that will emphasize what the role and duty of the Blackman and woman so that they can get back on track with God and leave this World of Sin. Why must women be shown their true selves? Because Women are lost! They are living a life of Death; Abortion, Prostitution, Murder, Lying, Cheating, Stealing and if something is not done by God, then the Woman could lose her Identity altogether. Her true identity is a help-mate to the Man, a lover, a companion, a wife, a friend, and a mother. This does not mean that she is estranged from financial, educational, legal, or any domestic relationship within the community. She has her place and the Man has his place within the scheme of the society. The true image of the woman is supportive, and her place is wherever she is needed.

In conclusion, her place is helping the poor, feeding the sick, making money in the workplace, doing chores in the home, child rearing, loving her children and husband. There are No-Off Limits to the Woman as long as there is a need in the community and she is supportive in her role as the Mother of Civilization. The greatest problem to the Blackwoman being her true self is the Mind that she has "Acquired" living in America. This Mind of Sin is attracted to Foolishness, Indecency, Mischief, Adultery, Lying, Fornication, and all the other vices that are in America.

PART I.

THE WHITEMAN'S IMAGE OF CIVILIZATION WAS TAUGHT TO HIM BY THE BLACKMAN!

Making Of A New Man

Let Us Make A "New" Man In Our Image.

(Genesis 1: 26-27) And God said, Let "Us" make Man in our image, after "Our" likeness and let "Them" have dominion over the fish of the sea, and over the earth, and over every creeping thing that creepeth upon the earth. So God created Man in his own image, in the image of God created he him, male and female created he them. The explanation of this scripture is :God said Let "Us" make man in our image. The "Us" is the Black Nation making the Races through a process of Birth Control. Let "Them" have dominion over the earth. Each Race is to rule the earth for a period of time (Brown, Red, Yellow and White).The Whiteman is the "New Man destined to rule for 6,000 years according to his own character and behavior. The Blackman is the father of the Races (All Races).

Man produces Man, like Sheep produces Sheep, and Birds produces Birds. Each species produces after its own kind.The birth control process was simply restrictive marriage by color only. The darker people could not marry a dark one and the lighter one kept marrying lighter and lighter, until there were a different race (Brown), then the process continued until the last stage which is White. According to scripture the process took 600 years to complete on the Isle of Patmos in the Aegean Sea .

Revelation 1:9,11-14. Scientifically, many feel that Natural Selection is the process of how the Races were produced. The Blackman left the fertile crescent of the Nile River in Africa, and explored the planet traveling through Europe then along the Bering Strait, on through China, and down to Australia, and South, Central and North America, back to Europe and Africa.

Where ever the Blackman traveled, he left a remnant of people, the people in Alaska called themselves Eskimos, China called Chinese, South, Central, and North America people were called Indians, Europeans called Caucasian. Natural Selection means that a race remove the undesirable characteristics like melan, diet, or climatic condition that will hinder its survival.

That is why each race look different because nature provides this mechanism of change wherein a species can adapt to an environment for survival. This also explains that there is only "One Nation on Earth and that is the Human Nation because all human beings have their origin in God." However, this must be made clear how God evolved the Races.

Making Of A New Man

The spiritual dispensation that the world is living under now is "Let Us Make A New Man" and give him six-thousand years to rule the earth and all that is on it. The new man is a Man that must rule with Unrighteousness, in order to test the people's will as to how they were created; the people were created Righteous by Nature. Mankind was given six days to do his work (A day with God is 1,000 years). The seventh day he must rest from his work, which means at the beginning of the 7,000 year, his work is completed; although the next ruler (Blackman) will be establishing his future world while Mankind's world will began to disintegrate.

The point is that this world of evil will cease time-wise (the 6,000 years of rulership will be up in 1914) but they will still be in power until a stronger society or God can replace them. Genesis 3:3 The first recorded "fall from grace" took place with Adam and Eve in the Garden, wherein God the friut of the tree which is in the midst of the Garden, Ye shall not eat of it, nor shall ye touch it lest ye die. 3:4 And the serpent said unto the woman, ye shall not surely die. 3:6 She took of the fruit thereof, and did eat, and gave also her husband with her; and he did eat. The true meaning of this parable is that the Tree of the Knowledge of Good and Evil was the two different ways of life, and they were to refrain from the Evil way of Life.

4

The serpent was their lower passion or desires talking to them (illicit sex and carnal behavior), and they turned their back to God's way of life and chose the wrong way of life, Scriptually, the name Adam and Eve means "A NewBeginning" and when Adam and Eve are mentioned, it only means the first or a new beginning of something. There have been many thousands of Adam and Eve's because there have been many new beginnings since the world began. However, the current Adam and Eve that is been discussed is Mankind, which consist of the White Race.

Remember, the prophecy is Let "Them" (The New Adam and Eve) have dominion over the earth for 6,000 years. The first two thousand years from (6,000 to 4,000 BC.) witnessed a decline in the power of the Blackman to rule, and a rise in the power of the Orientals in the East. From 4,000 to 3,000 BC. when the Caucasians were rising out of the caves of Europe.

WHITEMAN KNOW THYSELF!

The history of the Whiteman and his civilization does not go back any further than 6,000 accorded to recorded time. There is no records of when time began for the Blackman because there was no one there to record his coming into existence. He was the first Man.

5

Know Thyself Whiteman

The only evidence of time is artifacts, bones, or other antropological evidence dating into the millions and millions of years. This period that we are living in is known as the Whiteman's history or the period that scripture refers to as Let Us Make Man In Our Image. The Blackman has allowed the Whiteman to rule the world as a Test to his righteousness and ability to progress. He has done a poor job in every area of human relations, air pollution, human health is at an all time low, moral decay, and robbing the human family of the knowledge of God.

Once the New Man was made, through a process of Restrictive Birth Control, the Whiteman was living in the East among the black people as one of their own. They started making trouble among the Righteous Black people through telling lies, backbiting, and trouble-making. The Black People were living a moral life and could not understand the source of all the confusion until the authorities determined that it was the Caucasians or "New People" that was causing all the trouble. They made the Caucasians to take off their shoes off their feet and to walk twenty-two hundred and fifty miles across the Arabian Desert, into the Caves of West Asia which is now called Europe

There they lived for two thousands years in the hard and changeable climate of Europe. Many of them died in the desert, and when they got across the desert into the Caves of Europe. They went Savage.

They lived in the "Caves" of Europe. This name Eu-rope, Eu means hillsides and caves, and rope means to bind in. Which the Blackman did; they were put in the caves of Europe and roped in, Meaning, that the Straits were fortified by connecting the Sea of Marmara with the Aegean Sea that separates the Gallipoli Peninsula from Asia Minor called the Dardanelles and filled it with mines or high explosives, so that if they tried to come back into Asia, all that is needed is just explode the mine and destroy the intruders.

The Whiteman lost the knowledge of himself and civilization and went totally savage. He raised his family in holes and in caves. He did not know about building homes for himself, and after a thousand years was walking on his all fours (hands and Feet). At night, he would sleep in trees and watch the entrance of the cave where his family was and keep the wild animals from coming in and destroying his family. Their wives Mammalia (had sex) with the dogs in this savage state, and this is still going on today. The dog was tamed and became their best weapon against the will beast. The dog was loved by the fanily and became known as "Man's Best Friend."this come from the cave days.

The Monkey Family came from the Whiteman co-habitating with the beasts and living a savage life. There was not a monkey on the planet before this period of the Whiteman living a savge life in the caves of Europe.

7

Know Thyself Whiteman

There was not any difference in the way they lived 4,000 years ago than a beast or animal. Only they were of human origin. They ate all kind of poison foods, like they do now, only they ate more raw food than they do now. They started going Nude and became shameless, like they do today. Remember, they were in this condition for two-thousand years before Moses was sent to them to raise them up to rule, by teaching them the Art of Civilization . This is the real history of the Whiteman before he build up Europe and the Government that eventually was to rule the world for a period of time.

Moses became their God and leader. He brought them out of the caves and taught them to believe in God. How to walk and how to talk. How to wear clothes. How to cook food. How to season it with salt and what beef they should kill to eat. How to use fire for their service. Moses taught them against putting the female cow under burden. He established Friday as the day to eat fish, and not to eat beef on that day. Fish is the main menu in many of their home today on Friday. They were so evil (savage) that Moses had to build a ring of fire around him at night, and he would sleep in the middle of the ring to keep them from harming him. They were afraid of fire and still are today.

Moses taught the Whiteman that if he (they) would follow and obey him that they would Rule the world. Most of them believed Moses just to get out of the caves.

They were given the knowledge and power to bring every living thing , regardless of its kind , into subjection. And God said Let Us Make Man In Our Image after our Likeness, Let them have dominion over the fish of the sea, and over the fowl of the air, and over the cattle, and over all the earth and subdue it. (Genesis 1:26-28) The above was necessary if they (Whiteman) was to rule as a God of the world. They must conquer and bring into subjection all life upon the earth- not land life alone, but they must subdue the sea, master everything including the human family until a Greater God comes on the Seventh Day (7,000 year) which would mean the end of their time and power to rule over the earth and the human family.

This is the" New Man "that God had Moses to make to Rule the world for 6,000 years --The Whiteman! He has 4,000 more years to go. The Religion that Moses taught them to practice is Judaism. They are not the original Jews because the original Jews are Black People, but this is the Religion that they were given to practice as a Way of Life. Moses was an original Blackman and Prophet.

Socrates. Plato, Aristotle were educated by the Blackman.

The foundation for self-knowledge is the University and the oldest known university on earth is located in Cairo, Egypt. From this great institution of learning came scholars from all over the world to learn about life. All of the learned men from Europe like Socrates, Plato, Aristotle came and was taught by the Blackman of the east. They went back to their own society and became known as the Father of this science wherein the real Father of that science was in the Blackman. Here are some examples !

1. Ethiopians gave the world the first idea of Right and Wrong and thus laid the foundation for Religion.
2. The Bible originated in ancient Egypt; taken to Europe and translated into Hebrew and Greek texts, then translated into the English version known as the King James Version of the Bible.
3. The Whiteman took the King James Version with all the people looking white and claimed to be God's people and the representative of scripture.
4. Hannibal was a full blooded Blackman and the father of military strategy and it is being taught at West Point Military School today, however, he is not given credit, and in the movies he is portrayed as some whiteman. I wonder why?

5. The Father of Medicine was a blackman named Imhotep who lived in ancient Egypt in 2300 BC. and was the Doctor of Medicine to King Zoser. The Greek medicine men used to travel to the Middle East getting knowledge of medicine from him and he was the father of the phrase "Eat, Drink, and Be Merry for tomorrow you die." Now, 2000 years later a European named Hippocrates is called the Father of Medicine and the Hippocratic Oath must be administered before one can become a Doctor of Medicine, I wonder Why?

My point for mentioning the origin of the Bible, Medicine, Military Science is to show that not only has the Whiteman distorted history but he has denied the Blackman what is rightfully his: The Knowledge of his True Self. There is nothing wrong with the whiteman uplifting himself in his own society, but to hide where you got certain knowledge and use it as your own is a crime.

Socrates 470-399 B.C. A Greek Teacher and Philosopher

A society is only as strong as its educational system. In Athens, Greece Socrates was the greatest Philosopher and teacher of his time. He was married with children but he did not support them because all he did was teach young children in the Athenaeum about life. His philosophy was Know Thyself and then be true to thine self. SOCRATES WAS GAY OR A HOMOSEXUAL.

11

The authorities at the time felt that he was corrupting the youth (Sexually) and condemned him to death if he did not stop his impious acts; he refused and drank the poisonous hemlock rather than compromise his principles. Athens Greece (city-state) was the fore-runner of Democracy in European society , and the American Government is patterned after its institutions and Way of Life. In Athens, citizens discussed laws, nature, philosophy, and they deviated from the Divine Laws of God if they did not agree. This is Democracy!

Throughout Europe, for the past seventeen hundred years, the Europeans had been living according to the laws of God as taught by Moses. However, a complete break was taking place three hundred years before the advent of Jesus Christ. In Nineveh, a king named Nimrod allowed his people to grow further and further from the Laws of God, he was very evil and he made wars and revolutions for many years. He was so wicked that he made love to his mother (Sexually), He was born December 25, and when he died, his mother buried his body behind the castle near a tree , and every December 25th she would place gifts under the tree celebrating his birth.

When Jesus Christ died, the Jews were aware of this practice of Nimrod's mother, so for commercial reasons they told the Christians that Jesus was born on December 25th.

Thus, In order to celebrate his birth they should buy gifts for one another, place them under a tree, open them on Christ-mas, in recognition of their savior. However, the Christians are not celebrating the birth of Jesus but rather the birth of Nimrod the Wicked. (I wonder why this trick was toldand practiced the world-over?) The reason is because the very foundation of European society is based on tricks and lies to achieve power over the darker nations of earth. It is time to enter into the modern era of Jesus Christ (A Blackman from the East that was sent to the European Jews to convert them back to Righteousness as taught by Moses). Matthew 5:17 Think not that I am come to destroy the law, or the prophets; I am not come to destroy, but to fulfill.

CHAPTER II
JESUS: MATTHEW 6:24 YE CANNOT SERVE GOD AND MONEY!

In the year 331, Alexander The Great conquered Darius the Persian emperor and changed history. He wanted to establish a Eurasian state! However, he died and his scheme to amalgamate the Greeks with the Asians was implemented by widespread marriage of his troops with the black women of the east. The Jews (Blacks) that lived in Palestine would not accept Greek culture, nevertheless, the King Anthiochus was determined to Helenenize the Jews. Many Jews were killed, others fled to different countries and Egypt. Only those Jews that supported Anthiochus policies remained in Jerusalem.

The Greeks established holidays, Sabbath, Statues, and other observances that were contrary to the Jews and their Laws from God. The pig or hog was cooked near the Temple (the same as today), and the Jews that went along with these practices of the Greeks were the ones that Jesus was trying to correct and bring back to practicing the Laws of Moses.

In the year 65 BC. the Roman armies under Pompey captured Jerusalem and in 70 AD the Jewish state was completely destroyed. During this period, military Governors controlled Palestine, and many atrocities were committed against the black Jews. It is estimated that over 1,000,000 Jews fled into Africa, fleeing from Roman persecution and slavery.

14

The slaves market consisted of Black Jews evicted from their own homeland. The Jews that escaped went to Libya, Egypt, and Ethiopia. Deuteronomy. 28:64 And the Lord shall scatter thee among all people from the one end of the earth even unto the other; and there thou shall serve other gods, which neither thou nor thy fathers have known, even wood and stone . This is the condition that Jesus Christ was born (Black Sheep) a condition wherein his people were made slaves in their own land, could not worship their own God and were forced to be other than themselves. His life and history is an example of how things will be at the end of the Whiteman's time to rule over the Blackman.

At the time of Jesus' birth the population had become Eurasian or mixed with Asian and European ancestry, so the color is not as important as the tradition (Perpetuation of God's Laws) is practiced by his people. Jesus came to re-establish the Laws of God. Luke 1:26 And in the sixth month, the angel Gabriel was sent from God into a city of Galilee, named Nazareth. 27 To a virgin espoused to a man whose name was Joseph, of the House of David; and the virgin's name was Mary. 31 And behold, thy shall conceive in thy womb, and bring forth a son, and shall call his name Jesus. 34 And then said Mary unto the angel, How shall this be, seeing I know not a man? 35 And the angel answered and said unto her, The Holy Spirit shall come upon thee, and the power of the highest shall overshadow thee; Therefore also that holy thing which shall be born of thee shall be called the Son of God. 37 For with God nothing shall be impossible.

15

JESUS PEOPLE WERE CAPTURED MENTALLY BY MONEY AND FALSE VALUES.

When Jesus was born, the Jewish State of Palestine had been under captivity of the Roman Empire for almost 400 years and the prophecy was that a King would be born to liberate the Jews from their bondage, but Jesus was only a sign of what was to come 2,000 years later in America, at the end of Satan's time to rule over the Blackman.

Jesus real name was Ibin Yusef meaning the Son of Joseph, and his mother's name was Mary. According to the Bible, her espoused (husband) to be was Joseph and when the angel Gabriel made his announcement about taking care of the child, he would be blessed with the Holy Spirit--- He was speaking in the Future! This is why Mary was confused and said Howshall this be, seeing I know not a Man? The angel was preparing Mary and Joseph because the authorities would try to kill Jesus because they had anticipated someone being born among the Jews that would overthrow their government.

So Mary and Joseph were prepared for this event, and during Mary's pregnancy she was hid from the public, also the actual birth of Jesus was kept a secret in order to protect the child. NO ONE ACTUALLY KNOWS THE EXACT DATE OF JESUS BIRTH.

Jesus was a Prophet and God was his spiritual father and guide. Joseph was Jesus real physical father and Mary was his mother. He was born out of wedlock (Black Sheep) , Mary's father would not let her marry Joseph because he was a carpenter and commoner. Mary was well educated and her father a wealthy architect. But, they were in love with each other and this was how Jesus was conceived and born in secrecy to protect his life.

During the formative years, he spent his childhood around Nazareth and in Egypt with his father's people. He was educated like any other child and was an A student. Jesus did not know his future until a "Medium" told him who he was in scripture.

Jesus finished school at the age of twelve, this medium met Jesus coming from school and told him Who He Was in Scripture, and he taught him the knowledge of the "Radio In The Head" so that he could perceive messages and send messages when on his mission. He knew that the authorities would try to kill him and this Radio In The Head knowledge would protect him. He went home and told his mother and father everything and said" Luke 2:49 I must be about my father's business."

He left home at the age of twelve and spent twenty-two years on his mission of converting the Jews back to the Laws of Moses, he failed in his endeavor to convert the Jews back to righteousness, and was betrayed by one of his disciples.

17

However, this is only another example of Man's Fall from Grace because of Money, by one of Jesus' disciples named Judas Iscariot, Matthew 26:15 And said unto them, what will you give me, and I will deliver him unto you? And they bargained with him for thirty pieces of silver; the equal exchange was knowledge for thirty pieces of silver (Fool's Gold). Real Gold (Money) is the knowledge, skills, talents, and abilities of a people or individual to provide whatever physical things they want out of life.

Gold, minerals, or lumber is nothing if the person does not recognize it for what it is; it is the Mind of Man that gives it value because of its usefulness to him, if these physical items were of no usefulness to Man then they would have no value. The Only True Source of Wealth in the world is Knowledge and how an individual applies that Knowledge.

Fool's Gold is the opposite or counterfeit of real knowledge, it is deceitful knowledge, lies, or treachery that causes your Mind to see the Paper money, cars, or houses as the reward for your efforts, whereas the real reward is the ability, talent, or know-how that you have to support yourself. Judas's real gold was his discipleship with Jesus, but he sacrificed that for thirty pieces of silver (Fool's Gold).

However, it must be remembered the principle of Sacrifice and Redemption (Deliverance) Jesus sacrificed his life with service to God but he was not crucified on the cross, he was delivered. Holy Quran 4-157 plainly states We have killed the Messiah, Jesus, son of Mary, the messenger of Allah, and they killed him not, nor did they cause his death on the cross, but he was made to appear to them as such, and certainly those who differ therein are in doubt about it. They have no knowledge about it, and they killed him not for certain. The Gospel contains clear testimony that Jesus Christ escaped death on the cross. The following points may be noted.

1. Jesus remained on the cross for a few hours only (Mark 15:25 - John 19:14)

2. The two men crucified with Jesus was still alive when taken down from the cross; the presumption is that Jesus was alive .

3. The breaking of legs was resorted to in the case of the two criminals but was dispensed with in the case of Jesus (John 19:32-33).

4. The side of Jesus being pierced, blood rushed out, and this was a certain sign of life.

5. Pilate did not believe actually believe that Jesus died in so short a time (Mark 15:44).

6. Jesus was not buried like the two criminals, but was given into the charge of a wealthy disciple of his, who lavished care on him and put him in a spacious tomb hewn in the side of a rock (Mark 15:46).

7. When the tomb was seen on the third day, the stone was found to have been removed from its mouth (Mark 16:4) which would not have been the case if this had been a supernatural resurrection from the grave.

8. Mary saw him and took him for a gardener.

9. Jesus wore a disguise, and such disguise would not have been needed if he had rise from the dead.

10. Jesus was in the same body of flesh and his wounds were deep enough for a person to thrust his hand in (John 20: 25-28).

11. Jesus undertook the journey to Galilee with two of his disciples walking side by side
with him which shows that he was fleeing from refuge. A journey to Galilee was not necessary to rise to heaven (Matthew. 28:10).

Jesus prayed the whole night before his arrest to be saved from the accursed death on the cross, and he also asked his disciples to pray for him. The prayers of a righteous man in distress and affliction are always accepted and answered by God. Jesus had Sacrificed and his prayers were answered and he was Redeemed (delivered from the cross). The Rise and Fall of the Blackman is due to his Sacrificing his life in the service of God and his being Redeemed or Delivered from his Sins, or whatever has him in bondage (Sex or Money).

The emperor Aurelius Constantine accepted Jesus' teachings that had become so popular and converted to Christianity , he made it the state religion, and in 325 AD at the Council of Nicaea, the Nicene Creed was re-written to reflect in all the teachings of Christianity that Jesus Christ was God in human flesh. THIS BECAME OFFICIAL CHURCH DOCTRINE TO THIS VERY DAY! Jesus mission was "Luke 19:10 To Save That Which Was Lost" which was the Black Jews that were lost in the Roman Way of Life, and his mission was to Return them to the Fold of the teachings of Moses; they were referred to as a Lost Sheep. Jesus had learned that you cannot Reform A Devil because he must Be Born Again Spiritually in order to return to God.

PROPHET MUHAMMAD CAME TO FREE HIS PEOPLE FROM IDOL-WORSHIP!

Six hundred years after Jesus, Muhammad Ibin Abdullah was born in Mecca, Arabia. At the age of forty, he received his commission from God to preach the word "There is no God but Allah and Muhammad is his Messenger. He preached this message for over twenty-three years and at the end of his ministry, he had delivered to the world the Glorious holy Quran. Jesus gave the world the Gospel after twenty-two years. Thus it is important to realize that a true Prophet always deliver a scripture to the people that he represents.

Moses gave the Jewish people the Torah which contains all of the traditions, laws, and Beliefs of the Religion. First, the Torah, then the Gospel, and now the Holy Quran. Prophet Muhammad said that this book (Quran) was the final guide given to Man before the destruction of this world of Satan.

Muhammad learned in his message that he received from God that the Europeans were the cause of much of the trouble on the planet earth, and that they must be destroyed. If it had not been for a revelation telling him that they had 1,400 years more to live, then he would have killed them all. He drove most of them out of the Holy Land and established Islam as the dominant religion.

The knowledge that he was 1,400 years too soon to destroy the devils weaken his heart and he died at the age of 63 years. He gave the world the Holy Quran , and the Seed of Abraham, that was originally to build the Kingdom of God has now been taken away from the Jews and given to another i.e. the Muslims. Read Holy Quran Chapter 18, titled The Cave.

Some features of the Holy Quran and its Prophets are : Abraham, Moses, Noah, Jesus, and Muhammad; all are prophets of God, and all were considered as Black Sheep to their people before being accepted by their people. They all represented a Truth from God to a people at one time or another. The Christians claim that the prophets are their own, but this is not true because Prophets are always born among the people that they are sent to teach. They are one of the people. God established it this way so that the people cannot claim that they did not understand his speech, language, or dress code, or some reason to reject him. The Prophet looks, acts, dress, eat the same food, just like the downtrodden people he was commissioned to uplift.

Abraham was sent to his people, Noah was sent to his people, Moses was sent to his people, Jesus was sent to his people, and Muhammad was sent to his people. No Prophet was ever sent to White People because they killed the Prophets.

Some of the principles of Islam are:

Prophet Muhammad

1. Belief in One God whose proper name is Allah.
2. The Belief in all the Prophet from Abraham , Noah, Moses, Jesus, and Muhammad and the scripture that they bring. i.e.. Torah, Gospel, Holy Quran, and Psalms.
3. Charity in all of its forms, material as well as spiritual.
4. Prayer and Fasting
5. Hajj , a pilgrimage to Mecca to visit the Kabba once in the lifetime of a Muslim.

The purpose of Prophet Muhammad's life was to bring the Holy Quran to the world and now it must be fulfilled by establishing the Kingdom of God on earth as a reality. The Man that is to come and establish the Kingdom is known as the "Second Coming of Jesus" and his wisdom will set in motion the Kingdom that will be known as the Kingdom of God. In the meantime the Holy Land will be re-taken by the Europeans until the end of Satan's time to rule in 1914, or 1400 more years.

Remember, Muhammad's mission was to return the people to worshipping One God like Abraham and Ishmael had established, but the people had strayed to Idolatry, so another Messenger was necessary to return the people back to God. Muhammad re-captured the Holy City of Mecca, and converted much of the population to Islam, but he died at the age of sixty-three and 1/2 years because he tried to Reform the Europeans that were living in the area.

24

The old scientist use to laugh at him because history teaches that You cannot Reform A Devil, Black or White, he must be Born Again. He failed, and there are many wise people today who do not know the difference between being Converted to God, and Being Born Again in God. A Righteous person By Nature can be Converted to God if he strays away from God. However, an Unrighteous Person by Nature must be Born Again within his nature to Return to God.

Again, Jesus said to Nicodemus John 3:3-6 Verily, Verily I say unto thee, Except a man be born again, he cannot see the Kingdom of God. 6 That which is born of flesh is flesh, and that which is born of the spirit is spirit. (Study the nature of these two people "Black and White" and see which is born of the flesh, and which is born of the spirit. Study the nature of a person's behavior and make your own decision.

After 1,000 years of being locked up in Europe the Caucasians or Europeans were loosed out of their confinement to roam around the earth, causing all kinds of havoc and destruction. The Bible states it this way, Revelation Ch-20 7-8   7 And when the thousand years are ended Satan shall be loosed out of his prison, 8 And shall go out to deceive the nations which are in the four quarters of the earth, Gog and Magog to gather them together to battle; the number of whom is as the sand of the sea.

Prophet Muhammad

The Holy Quran mention it this way Chapter 18, verse 94 They said: O Dhu-l-qarmain, Gog and Magog do mischief in the land. May we then pay thee tribute on condition that thou raise a barrier between us and them? The ancestors of the present Teutonic and Slav races are the Gog and Magog spoken in the Holy Quran. Gog and Magog are described as two nations whose depredations on peaceful nations were brought to an end by Darius, but will later be let loose out of their confinement and dominate the whole world. Gog and Magog or the European nations , having subdued the whole world could not agree on the division of the spoils(Money), and they are at one another throats, and this struggle has assumed the form of world conflict.

One World War ends only to be followed by another. Matthew 24: 7-8 states the circumstances of the time at the end of Satan's rule, Nations shall rise against nations, and Kingdom against Kingdom: And there shall be famines, and pestilence, and earthquakes, in divers places. All these are the beginning of sorrows.

The word slave originates from the "Slavs" which means to bound one in servitude, after capturing him, Slavs are white people from eastern Europe. Human efforts will not be able to restore the balance to the world, but a mighty revolution is going to come about that will unite Man into a spiritual Faith that will enable him to see that there is only one nation on earth and that is the Human Nation.

The current identity of Gog and Magog that is controlling the world is ; Gog is the United States of America and Magog is the Union of Soviet Socialist Republic, they have always been brothers and one controls the Eastern part of the world and the other controls the Western portion. Now, we enter into the last 400-500 years of Satan's rule over other nations.

After the Whiteman's time to rule is up, he will still be in power until the Blackman is able to Resurrect his Mind, Identity, Nation, all of the essential ingredients that makes a people self-sufficient. As this Resurrection takes place world-wide, you will witness the relinquishing of territories, land, cultures, and societies back to the Blackman. THIS IS HAPPENING NOW! Let us go the next step, and find out what prevents Man from enjoying heaven on earth.

CHAPTER III.
THE DEVIL IN MAN
(lower Passions)

Holy Quran 51: 47-49 And the heavens, we raised it high with power, and We are Makers of the vast extent, and the earth, We have spread it out. How well we prepared it! And of everything we have created pairs that you may be mindful. In God's creation, we are told that everything is created in pairs. There are pairs in the animal world, the vegetable world, and in the world of human beings. In fact, the heavens and the earth is considered a pair because of how they interrelate and creates a whole. In the case of the Blackman, and his creation, he is a pair or dual being. Two ventricles equals the heart, Right and left Cerebral Hemisphere equals the Brain, Two arms and legs for balance, and so forth throughout the body until the human being is complete.

There is one law operating throughout the human system and that is the Law of Evolution. This law has purpose and wisdom, behind it's purpose is to foster or bring up the individual, nourish, regulate the being, complete the growth cycle, and accomplish whatever idea is in the Mind of the person. Thus, the law operating within the human being is to make the person attain to one condition after another until it reaches it 's goal of perfection. THIS IS THE WAY EVERYTHING IN LIFE WORKS!

Now, the Devil in the Blackman and Whiteman is simply the way they were created by God. Remember, Man is a dual being. God created Man with two kinds of passions, the higher passions awaken in him the spiritual life or Godly life. The lower passions which relates to his physical life, when out of control leads to thinking and acting like an animal. These two types of passions are referred to as being of God or of the Devil. The word Devil means that which is contrary to God and his way of life.

The lower passions are necessary for man's physical life but is a hindrance to him when out of control. The Blackman is required to keep these passions under control. If he does this, then they will become a help to him instead of a hindrance in his advancement. "THE LOWER PASSIONS OR DESIRES IN THE MAN IS HIS DEVIL! Some lower passions are Envy, Jealousy, Murder, Lying, Stealing, Chicanery, Backbiting, Robbery, and Deception. The Thought and Action equals Devil, this is the dark side of Man's nature.

However the flip side of Man's nature is Divine; he is the creator of civilization, the developer of the sciences, and the founder of civilized behavior like wearing clothes, rules of society, good manners, and civility. Living according to his higher desires produces Wisdom, Kindness to your fellow man, Peace of Mind, Contention of Mind, Friendships throughout the world, and Goodwill to All Men.

Devil In Man

This is the behavior that can be practiced daily and will eliminate or control the Devil within. The question was asked Prophet Muhammad Ibin Abdullah "Do You have a Devil?" His reply was yes, but Allah has helped me to overcome him so he has submitted and does not command me aught but good." The prophet's devil had submitted to him and instead of making evil suggestions to his mind, he became a help in the development of his higher life because he no longer was hindered by his lower passions or Devil .

Man has the ability to talk to himself (Soliloquy), and when scripture mention that the Devil talked to Adam in the Garden of Eden it was Adam or Man entertaining doubt in his mind about which course of life to take. The Devil or his Lower Passions won out according to the story of Adam and Eve, and thus brought about the first "Fall from Grace" The Devil refusing to submit to Man or the God in Man is the fight that goes on within the human being until the Higher or Lower way of life becomes the norm for the human being.

To repeat, the Devil is the lower passions that dwells in Man, and the story of Adam and Eve in the Garden is an illustration of whether Man and Woman will make the right decision and choose to live according to the Higher Passions or God within them , or the choose the wrong course of life and live according to their lower passions or Devil.

MARRIAGE and FREE LOVE

Marriage is the basic principle of human civilization. Marriage is the union of two natures which are one in essence. man and woman were created from each other." Holy Quran 4:1O people keep your duty to your Lord, Who created you from a single being and created its mate of the same(kind), and spread from these two many men and women. 42:11 The Originator of the Heavens and earth. He has made for you pairs from among yourselves. 16:72 And Allah has made wives for you from among yourselves, and has given you sons and daughters from your wives, and has provided you with good things. It is obvious from these scriptures that man and woman were created for each other, and marriage is the institution that brings them together to God. Marriage does not consist of a Man and Man, or a Woman and Woman in the sight of God.

One of the object of marriage is the multiplication of the human race. Many detractors of marriage would say that the human race could be multiplied without the institution of marriage, and this would only be accepted if Man lived his life like an animal. Just roaming the earth having children without the aid of society or civilization to nurture, nourish, and care for the infants to maturity. No respect for one another, or your obligation, or the rights of others would reduce Man to being an animal or brute in human form, and without civilization and the institution of marriage, before long there would be no human race at all.

Marriage

It takes Law and Order to preserve human life and dignity. Next, without marriage, there can be no family, no kinship, or a force unifying the different elements of humanity together; It is through the family that humanity is held together and civilization made possible, and marriage creates the legal family. Love and service is developed through marriage. The institution of marriage is responsible for the development of feelings of love and service, because Love is not based on a momentary passion but a lifelong connection.

The home is the first training ground of love and service. The natural inclination of the male to the female, and of the female to the male finds expressions through marriage and is developed , first, into a love for the children, then a love for one's kith and kin, and ultimately into disinterested love for the whole of humanity. Prophet Muhammad Ibin Abdullah said: " The best of you is he who treats his wife best".

Free Love (Free Sex)

Free Love is becoming more the "norm" in the Western cultures and societies instead of marriage. This will prove to be disastrous and the ruin of western civilization. Marriage is being discarded not because there is an inherent flaw, but because it has certain responsibilities within the contract for both parties to adhere. These responsibilities are the cause of avoiding marriage. Marriage requires that each party share in their sorrows as well as their pleasures.

Free Love makes each partner extremely selfish, because while they are partners in happiness, each is free to leave the other , uncared for, in his or her sorrow. Marriage make each mate jointly responsible for the welfare of the children, but in Free Love, when either of the parents has had his/her satisfaction of the other, the children may be left without a shelter, or the procreation of children is avoided, thus the end that nature has for the union of man and woman is defeated. Free Love (Sex) opens the way to loose relations of the sexes, and entails no responsibility of any kind of the father for the care and bringing up of the children, who with the mother might be destitute. Occasions may arise for the dissolution of a marriage, and it will continue to arise as long as human nature is what it is (good and evil), but the answer is Divorce and not Free Love.

A union of the sexes with the acceptance of the consequent responsibilities is called marriage, and without the acceptance of responsibilities it is called fornication. There are some marriages that are forbidden; Holy Quran 4:23   Forbidden to you are your mothers, and your daughters, and your sisters, and your paternal aunts, and your maternal aunts, and brother's daughters and sister's daughters, and your mothers that have suckled you, and your foster sisters, and mothers of your wives, and your stepdaughters who are in your guardianship (born) of your wives of whom you have gone in - but if you have not gone into them, there is no blame on you- and the wives of your sons who are of your own loins; and that you should have two sisters together, except what has already passed.

Surely Allah is ever Forgiving, Merciful. These are the obvious people not to marry, but there is another religious admonition that must be addressed, and that is the idolater. The idolater is a person that worships idols, stones, statues, or images of another human being. An idolater idolizes or adores another person over God and his words. A man is admonished not to marry an idolater until she becomes a believer (regardless of faith). A believing maid is better than an idolater even though she pleases you; and do not give believing women in marriage to idolaters until they believe.

MUTUAL RELATION BETWEEN HUSBAND AND WIFE!

In the vast organization of a nation, there is someone to exercise the final authority in certain cases, so it is in the smaller organization of the home that there is a same arrangement. Thus, the husband is spoken of as being a ruler over" the people of the house", and the wife is described as " a ruler over the house of her husband and his children. The home is a kingdom in miniature where authority is exercised by both husband and wife. Unless one is given a higher authority, there would be chaos in the home. The reason for giving Man the authority over women is found in the Holy Quran 4:34 Section 6: Disagreement between Husband and Wife.

Men are the maintainers of women, with what Allah has made some of them to excel others and with what they spend out of their wealth. So the good women are obedient, guarding the unseen as Allah has guarded. And (as to) those on whose part you fear desertion, admonish them, and leave them alone in the beds and chastise them. So if they obey you, seek not a way against them. Surely Allah is ever Exalted, Great. The meaning is this:

1. Maintainer means that he maintain her and managed her affairs.

2. Obedience means obedience to Allah and his words.

3. Guarding the Unseen is a euphemism for guarding the husband's rights.

4. The two qualifications of a good wife is her piety or obedience to God and chastity.

5. Desertion means rising, or immoral conduct against her husband, or taking up an abode he does not like; the remedy for this is three-fold.

6. The remedy for a wife's desertion is : (a) She is only to be admonished (b) If she persist in the wrong course, separate from her bed.   (c) If she still persist, then chastisement is permitted as a last resort. (No striking or ill-treatment permitted). Chastisement can take many forms such as financial denial, restriction of privileges, and lack of personal contacts until the disagreement is solved. These remedies can be used by the husband or the wife.

WORK

The function of the husband and wife are distinct, and each is entrusted with functions which are best suited for his or her nature. God has made man and woman to excel each other the man in certain respect. The man excel the woman in constitution and physique, which is capable of bearing hardships and facing greater dangers than the physique of the woman. On the other hand, the woman excels the man in the qualities of love and affection. The woman is suited to bring up the children because of her preponderance of the quality of love in her. However, this is only a general rule, because women are not excluded from any activity of work.

The husband is required to earn a living for the maintenance of the family, and the wife is responsible for the management of the household and the bringing up of the children. The husband is bound to maintain his wife according to his means. The wife is to keep company with her husband, to preserve the husband's property from loss or waste, and to refrain from doing anything which should disturb the peace of the family. She is required not to admit anyone into the house whom the husband does not like, and not to incur expenditure of which the husband disapproves. She is not bound to render personal service such as the cooking of food, but the respective duties of the husband and wife are such that each must be ready to help each other. The wife must help the husband in the field if necessary, and the husband must help the wife in the household duties.

36

In the struggle of life, the intermingling of the two sexes cannot be avoided. However, unnecessary mingling of the sexes is discouraged. In some situations, a woman should not be alone in private with a man (private meetings). But when other people are also present, or one is exposed to public view there is no harm in being alone.

The object of limiting the intermingling of the sexes is to raise the moral status of society and to minimize the chances of illicit sexual relations growing up between the sexes, so that the home may be a haven of peace between the husband, the wife, and the children.

DIVORCE

In spite of the sacredness, the rights and responsibilities of marriage, sometimes under extreme circumstances the way must be kept open for its dissolution. The necessity for Divorce is recognized by all people. In fact, marriage is only a civil contract or agreement that two people will live together as husband and wife.

Divorce is the most hated of all things. It is a last resort in all cases. In a divorce the two parties are equal and on the same level. Divorces can be granted for Adultery, Incompatibility, Mental Cruelty, Physical Abuse, and Desertion. Divorce is viewed as a necessity in marital relations, because of the various conditions on the part of a husband and wife.

CHAPTER IV.
JOSEPH SOLD INTO SLAVERY

Before and during the time of Jesus Christ, slavery was an institution practiced by all people , and its primary end was economic gain, and not racial superiority. A father may sell his daughter into slavery to help support a family. Our story revolves around selling a boy into slavery because he was favored by God to become a leader of his people. Genesis 37:7 When Joseph was a lad of seventeen, he had a dream and he told it to his brothers.

He said, For behold, we were binding sheaves in the field, and lo my sheaf arose, and also stood upright; and behold your sheaves stood around about, and made obeisance to my sheaf. Joseph brothers hated and rejected him for this dream and they said, shall thou have dominion over us ? Joseph dreamed another dream and he told it to his brethren, and said behold I have dreamed another dream; and behold, the Sun Moon, and eleven Stars made obeisance to me. Joseph was from the land of Canaan, and Canaan gets its name from Noah's son Ham (who was black) and the founder of Canaan.

This land is known today as The Holy Land, The Land of Palestine, The Garden of Eden, and it was founded by a Blackman. Joseph and his brothers were Canaanites or Hamites and today we call them Africans.

Joseph father's name was Jacob and he was re-named Israel meaning "He Prevailed". The name Israel was to become the Spiritual Nation of God's People because they followed his laws, and prophets. THESE ARE BLACK PEOPLE AND NOT WHITE PEOPLE. Just as White people took Palestine during the time of Jesus, they also re-took Palestine in 1948, and named it Israel, although their behavior is an indication that they are not God's people because they will not obey his laws. In this modern day Israel, they have prostitution, gambling, liquor, murder, lying, and every vice imaginable, does this sound like God's Kingdom or God's People?

Although the Blackman is not holy today, his nature is still capable of establishing the Kingdom of God. Joseph's father, Isreal had made Joseph a coat of many colors, which symbolizes Joseph's mission of bringing together many different people of the earth. Joseph brothers plotted his death because of his dreams, and it came to pass that one day, Joseph was with his brothers, and they stripped Joseph of his coat, and cast him into a pit. They lifted up their eyes and said, look a company of Ishmaelites (Whites) going to Egypt (British Colonies).

Why kill him ? Let us sell him , and Joseph (Black Sheep) was sold into slavery (Another example of Man's fall from Grace for Money), the equal exchange was money for a servant (slave).

Sold into Slavery

Again,an example of exchanging "Real Gold" which was the wisdom of Joseph's dream of one day ruling a nation for "Fool's Gold" or cash money from the slave-traders.Joseph coat was smeared with the blood of an animal and taken to his father and he was told that he had been killed by an animal. The same is true of many black people who were kidnapped, and torn blood stained clothes given to parents who thought their children were killed by animals. Remember, the name Israel is a Spiritual name that represents God's people and their off-springs.

This story clearly shows that the Blackman of America is the offspring of Israel sold into slavery. Now let us see how Joseph vision of thehis brothers sheaves making obeisance to his sheaf, or the Sun, Moon, and eleven Stars bowing down to him becomes a reality in Egypt.

Genesis 37:36 And the Midianites sold him into Egypt unto Pot'iphar, an officer of Pharaoh's and captain of the guard. The Lord was with Joseph and he found favor in Pot'hpar's eyes and he made him overseer of the house and all that he owned. Everything that Joseph touched prospered and one day the master's wife cast her eyes upon Joseph 39:7 and she said Lie With Me (Sex) and Joseph refused. This went on day after day, until one day she caught Joseph by the coat and he ran leaving a portion of it in her hand. When her husband returned, he heard his wife loud cry that Joseph wanted to lie with her but she cried out and he fled leaving behind a piece of his garment.

Pot'iphar was outraged and cast Joseph into prison (Once again, the desire for illicit Sex the down-fall of Man). Remember, the Rise of Man is dependent on how he maintains the Laws of God during his crisis and stay within the Mental and Spiritual behaviors ordained by God.

JOSEPH FALSE ACCUSED OF SEXUAL ABUSE

At this point, spiritually, Joseph can be described as a Lost Sheep, outside the fold or community of God, although falsely accused, he held fast to his Faith in God. While in prison, the keeper of the prison found favor in Joseph because God was with him. He placed Joseph in charge of everything within the prison and one day the butler and baker (prisoners) dreamed a dream that they could not interpret, so they asked Joseph to interpret their dreams.

Genesis 40:5-23 The Butler dream was told to Joseph first: He said that a vine was before him and on that vine was three branches, and it budded, and her blossoms shot forth, and the clusters brought forth ripe grapes. Pharaoh's cup was in my hand, and I took the grapes and pressed them in Pharaoh's cup, and I gave the cup to Pharaoh. Joseph said the interpretation is: The three branches are three days, within three days, Pharaoh shall lift up thine head and restore thee unto thy place: and thou shall deliver Pharaoh's cup into his hand.

41

Sold into Slavery

Think of me when it shall be well with thee, and show kindness, make mention of me unto Pharaoh, and bring me out of this house. For indeed I was stolen away out of the land of the Hebrews: and here also have I done nothing that they should put me into the dungeon. The Baker saw that the interpretation was good so he told Joseph his dream. He said, I had three white baskets on my head, and in the uppermost basket there were all manner of food for Pharaoh; and the birds did eat them out of the basket upon my head.

Joseph said: The three baskets are three days, and within three days shall Pharaoh lift up thy head from off thee, and shall hang thee on a tree; and the birds shall eat thy flesh from off thee. And it came to pass, which was Pharaoh's birthday, that he made a feast unto all his servants. He lifted up the head of the Chief Butler and Chief Baker among his servants. He restored the chief butler unto his butlership and he gave the cup unto Pharaoh's hand. But he hanged the chief baker as Joseph had interpreted to them, yet the chief butler did not remember Joseph, but forgot him.

Spiritually speaking, Joseph represents the Blackman of America, who was stolen from his native land Africa, and brought to a foreign land (America) and sold into slavery. He was falsely accused by white women, killed castrated, and thrown into prison for no reason. While in prison (slavery)) for three hundred years or three days, his people abroad forgot about him (them).

They were considered dead by the other black nations of earth, so no-one searched for them. It came to pass that Pharaoh dreamed a dream and none of his magicians or wise men could interpret the dream, until the butler remembered Joseph in prison. Pharaoh sent for Joseph and told him his dream. He said I stood upon the bank of the river, and behold there came up out of the river seven cows, fat and well favored, and behold seven other cows came up after them, poor and very ill- favored, and they did eat the first seven fat cows. And when they had eaten them it could not be known that they had eaten them because they were still ill favored as in the beginning.

I saw in another dream , seven ears came up in one stark, full and good. And behold seven ears withered, thin, and blighted sprung up after them, and the thin ears devoured the seven good ears. Joseph said to Pharaoh that his dream was one dream related two different ways and not two different dreams. Joseph said, behold, there will come seven years of plenty throughout all the land, and after that will come seven years of famine. The famine shall consume the land because the famine will come after the years of plenty, so this is what must be done during the years of plenty.

1. Find a wise and discreet man to oversee the grain (Economic) collection and distribution.
2. Appoint officers through the land (City, State, Federal) to collect one-fifth of all the Food, Money, supplies, goods and materials

Sold into Slavery

3.Money during the plentiful years in the cities in preparation for the famine.

The time to prepare for hard times is always during the good times! Pharaoh was well pleased with Joseph and made him ruler over all of Egypt, second only to himself in command. Pharaoh placed a ring on Joseph finger, a gold chain around his neck , a chariot, re-named Joseph Zaph'enath-pane'ah, and he gave him as a wife Asenath, the daughter of Poti-phera, priest of On. And unto Joseph was born two sons before the famine came , the first born was named Manas'seh, meaning God has made me forget all my toil, and all my father's house. The name of the second called E'phraim, For God hath caused me to be fruitful in the land of my afflictions.

The seven years of plenty ended and the seven years of famine began. Spiritually speaking, America is styled as Egypt in this scripture, and although she has enjoyed some plentiful days as the nation's most powerful country on earth with plenty of bread (grain) to feed the world, hard times are coming. Look at Russia, starving for bread but there are plenty of bullets. When famine comes, it could be economic collapse, political instability or a food shortage. The point is that the Blackman (Joseph) who has been imprisoned, and mistreated will be the one whom God will bless with the wisdom to devise a strategy to save the nation, justWATCH AND SEE!

Joseph brothers came to buy grain but did not recognize their own brother. He sells them grain and devise a plan to re-unite his father Israel so that they can all bear witness to God's plan: To send him forward into slavery in order to save his people during a future crisis. GODIS A FORE-KNOWER. Joseph stood the test of faith and now was in a position to save his people. When Joseph revealed himself to his brothers and father, they were given portions of the land to dwell in and Israel was taken back to his own country to die, and Joseph and his off-springs dwelt in Egypt and he lived one hundred and ten years. Joseph died in Egypt (America) with the prophetic statement to his prodigy that God will bring you out of this land unto the land that he promised our fathers Abraham, Isaac, and Jacob (The Holy Land).

The conclusion to Joseph's story of being a Black Sheep is that although he was sold into because he dreamed that his brothers and their sheaves bowed downed to him, plus the Sun, Moon, and eleven Stars, showed obeisance to him, that this was all in God's plan of redeeming and saving their nation. The black sheep is sometimes lost to his mission until it is revealed to him like Moses, Jesus, and even Joseph. The point is that the Black Sheep stays true to his Faith in God and he will be delivered from his condition. Moses was delivered from Pharaoh, Jesus was delivered from the Cross (Believe It Or Not), and Joseph was delivered from Prison and saved the nation. A Joseph or Black Sheep will Rise among the People of America and save that nation in time of crisis.

CHAPTER V.

THE BLACKMAN AND WOMAN LOST THE KNOWLEDGE OF SELF IN AMERICA!

The Original Black People were tricked to America seeking Real Gold.

Real Gold is a precious metal that can be used for trade of other goods and services, also made into jewelry and is a status of wealth. Fool's Gold is a metal that has the appearance of fine gold in color, but it is not gold, only a worthless mineral. Many people are deceived out of their real wealth with Fool's Gold. Four hundred and Thirty Seven years ago, when the Whiteman of Europe was trading among our people in the East, he made an interpretation that in the new world there was real gold just lying on the ground, and all a person had to do was pick it up, come back home and be rich.

Many original black people (although wise) fell for this lie because the trader (John Hawkins) had gained their confidence, and also the scripture must be fulfilled wherein God's people would be lost in a strange land for 400 years. So, many got on the ship that was called the Good Ship Jesus, and once in America in 1555 (not 1619) they were made slaves. Once they realize that there was no Gold, they cried "You can have this Old world But just give me Jesus (The Good Ship Jesus), and today our people have made a spiritual song out of that bad situation.

What our people got was Fool's Gold or the appearance of something real . The Whiteman's Fool's Gold is what attracted us into slavery in the beginning and it is what is keeping us in slavery today. The Blackman is still seeking wealth and opportunity in the Whiteman's world instead of his own world. He left his real gold which is your own land, the knowledge of yourself and God, your own culture and history, language, and Flag; THAT IS REAL GOLD, metal in the ground is only a Symbol of the real wealth In Your Mind and Your Nation.

After this original trick, then the Whiteman set-up Trading Post all along the coast of Africa (rural areas) and started kidnapping, robbing, buying, and stealing every black person that they could find to help the labor force develop the New World. Black People are Still Developing The New World For The Whiteman. The Blackman's Real Gold was the physical, mental, and spiritual Image that he had of himself before been made a slave.

The whiteman gave a new mental and spiritual birth to the blackman called a Negro, Read Genesis 1:26 wherein He was given dominion over everything on the earth. But this was only for a short time, which would end spiritually in 1914, but mental slavery will continue as long as a people permit it to be, however, the time Divinely of 6,000 years is over! Revelation 13:18 states Here is Wisdom. Let him that hath understanding count the number of the beast; for it is the number of a man; and his number is six hundred--threescore--and six. 600,60,and 6, equals 666,000 or Six Thousand, Six-hundred and Six .

Fool's Gold

which means on the Sixth day (600 years) this man was made, he established the (6) six-day week to live by,and his time to rule the earth is for (6,000 years) was was up numerically in 1914. The time of the Blackman is (7) the Seventh thousand years of this dispensation, in which he comes back to re-claim his home, the planet earth. This Is Happening Now! The time periods can be counted in 2,000 year periods

The first 2,000 years were spent locked-up in Europe living the life of the Caveman . Moses came to them and taught them Civilization and this lasted for 2,000 years. Jesus came and tried to teach them and his teachings has lasted for 2,000 years up to now, which is a total of 6,000 years.

Now, can't you see the whiteman world falling apart, because his foundation for building it was on Slavery, Fool's Gold, and Deception.

BLACKMAN, WHO IS THAT MYSTERY GOD THAT YOU BELIEVE IN?

Mystery is anything that arouses curiosity because it is unexplained, inexplicable, or a secret. The original Blackman and Woman that was enslaved in America had the knowledge of God within themselves, and God was not a mystery to them. However, the offspring that were reared by White-people were given a vague, deceptive, and mysterious concept about God that is still prevalent today.

The babies of the original people were taught that God dwells in the sky and they would see him after they die; instead of the truth in scripture 1 Cor.3:16 Know Ye not that Ye are the Temple of God, and that the Spirit of God dwells in You? No human being sees God after he/she is physically dead because God is within that person while they are alive. To make contact with God, one must pray, and practice his word.

If God wants to make contact with you it is done by inner communication (intuition), outside communication (another person, nature, or through sending a Divine Messenger into the world explaining his purpose at that time,Abraham, Moses, Jesus, Muhammad and other prophets known and unknown). The point is that God is not a Mystery or a secret except to Black People who were mis-led by White people in slavery.

49

Mystery God ?

The Blackman must stop "Looking For God" (Mystery), and start "Being God" an actual state of mind in reality. The number one problem of the Blackman today is regaining his identity in God (Self). Once the location of God has been placed within the human being's creative mind then the person can identify with the source of his desires in life. For example, if the person wants a house then he can pray for guidance, financial direction, or assistance in purchasing a house. He would look for this assistance from within himself instead of looking to the sky.

All of the necessities of life like food, clothing and shelter comes from the earth and the mind of man, and not from the sky. GOD DWELLS WITHIN THE MIND OF MAN TO ASSIST HIM IN EVERYDAY LIFE, AND TO BE CLOSE TO HIS CREATION. GOD IS NOT SEPARATE FROM HIS CREATION, BUT "WITHIN" HIS CREATION. " Looking for A Mystery God" has caused the Blackman to be spiritually Blind, Deaf, and Dumb to himself and the powers that he posess to control his own destiny. He was made blind for a purpose and that purpose was to make a slave that looked to the whiteman for his every need and not look to God (Self).

This mystery God teachings is very dominant today in the churches of America, and has created a "Lock" on the minds of blacks that prevents them from progressing spiritually and will require Divine Truth from God to "Unlock" their minds from this mysterious concept of God.

50

A person's Spiritual Identity (God Within Self, Allah, Jesus, Etc.) is the first ingredient that is necessary in the building of their conception of self. Then this foundation is used to build their mentality or Mental Identity such as their culture, history, and name. Finally, there is a Physical Identity such as physical features like facial, hair, height, etc., finger-prints, and speech.

If these three separate identities are not clear to the individual about Who he Is and What he Believes, then he/she is operating from a mystery concept of God and Self. Now, when a person has a correct spiritual identity that is relative to their own culture, history, and name, then that person will Look Physically like a person from that culture, with that history, and having that name , which correspond with a Belief in that God and Way of Life.

The life-style of black people in America is not consistent with God' s Trinity of a consistent identity for Man. The identity is a mystery to himself, he believe in a White God (White Jesus) has a white name, born in a white culture and society, and have black features that he is constantly trying to re-make into white features. THIS PROCESS OF IDENTIFICATION WITH YOUR-SELF IS NOT NATURAL--IT IS MYSTERIOUS. Remember this, the Blackman was given guidelines or teachings (Overtly or Covertly) that taught him every phase or viewpoint on how to be a slave. The slave was given ideas about God that was not real.

51

Mystery God ?

The slave was given the wrong type of food to eat (mentally and physically), lies about his history i.e. swinging on trees instead of building civilization, The slave was taught to love, care, grieve, and protect white people. Also to mistrust, hate, backstab, and to fight his own self and kind, This is still a sad and

prevalent condition today. This Behavior is Not Godly, the slave must be taught How To Be A God. To be One with God, one must be convinced that the Spirit of God Dwells Within Self and then actualize this belief through your Way of Life. God means POWER or FORCE. This power must have a medium of expression and the human being is a carrier of this power for his own existence and well being. Thus, in order not to be led astray as to how to relate to God, it is important that this scripture be understood, which shows Jesus warning about mysterious teachings because if one is to ever see God, it must be in a Man. 1 Timothy 3:16 And without controversy great is the mystery of godliness: God was manifested in the flesh, justified in the Spirit, seen of angels, preached unto the nations, believed on in the world, received up into glory.

Colossians 2: 8 Beware lest any man spoil you through philosophy and vain deceit, after the tradition of men, after the rudiments of the world, and not after Christ. There is no logical or spiritual reasoning in this day and time (1995) to believe in a Mysterious or Mystery God. Jesus has made it plain that to see God is to see him in a Man, and to be Godly is to practice his laws.

PART II.
THE NEGRO WAS MADE IN THE IMAGE OF THE WHITEMAN.

In order to make a human being Think in A New Way about life, you must start re-educating the children or babies away from the original way that they had been educated. The Original Black people that landed in America were unable to educate or give the first knowledge to their off-springs of Who They Were, Their Culture, The Knowledge of their History or any-thing concerning their origin. The Whiteman took the children and mis-educated them by teaching them a false history, a false identity, and a false knowledge of their culture.

He told them that they were swinging on trees in Africa and he saved them, he told them that they had no name so they could use his name, he told them that God was in the shy and they would see him after they die. But the real weapon of the Whiteman was Fear. He instilled fear in the children , and black people grew up being afraid of the whiteman because he killed many blacks to instill this fear for him, and even today it has become a sub-conscious reaction whenever some blacks see a Whiteman. The reason some blacks still fear the whiteman is because they have been taught to eat the "Wrong Food" mentally and physically. The wrong food that cause fear is ignorance (Not Knowing the Truth) unable to provide for your sustenance in life, being dependent on others, eating Swine, drinking poisonous liquids (alcohol), not knowing who you are, it is these conditions that breeds Fear in the Blackman.

The average time span between a child becoming an adult is considered a generation (21 years) and it took about three generations for the Whiteman to produce a Grafted Mind-Set in the Blackman and Woman that was completely unintelligent, could not read or write, speak his language, could not comprehend religion, and was declared two-thirds a beast. This is what Whiteman did to the Blackman and Woman the first sixty-four years on the soil of America in order TO MAKE A SLAVE. The Minds of the children of the original Blackman and Woman was GRAFTED into the Minds of Slaves. Grafted means to Transplant from one state to another or to mix original knowledge with false knowledge and get a third diluted knowledge or Mind.

Grafting means to probagate a species or animal, or fruit by mixing an original product with another in order to produce an artificial product. For example, you mix an orange with a lemon and you can produce a grapefruit. The orange and lemon are natural fruits wherein the grape-fruit is artificial. You mix a horse with a donkey and you produce a mule. The horse and donkey are nature's animals but the mule is sterile and artificial or produced by mankind.

There are artificial vegetables, animals, shoes, or anything that you can think of the Whiteman has made some version of it in order to fulfill the scripture of Making A New World. He was to duplicate everything that the Blackman had created previously. His world Is Grafted and Unnatural and has come to an end.

54

The Blackman and Woman must be re-educated to the fact that their minds have been Grafted into a Slavery Mind or perspective on life and just as it took continuous education and suffering to get in this state, it will take re-education into Divine Knowledge to bring them back to their original conception of life. This Grafted Mind has produced Stealing, Murder, Insanity, Homosexuality, Lying, Grief, Sorrow, and Misery to the Black Community.

In order for the Whiteman to build his world as stated in Genesis 1:28 Be Fruitful and Multiply, have dominion over everything on earth, he has used Slavery as his number one tool and then he Grafts or transplant his way of thinking into the organism or human and produce a New Person, Nation, Fruit, Animal, or System.

Look over the earth and see how many nations are mixed up including the Blackman and woman of America. All because this New Man had to make a new world and he did it by Grafting. Grafting means to mix to different original products together and the third product is artificial and grafted. This artificial product (Whiteman and his world) is what we are living under today and not the world of God.

SIXTY-FOUR YEARS TO MAKE A NEGRO!
(Creating A Slave 1555-1619)

(THE INSTRUCTIONS OF A WHITE SLAVE-OWNER)

Let Us Make A Slave. What do we need ? First of all we need a black nigger man, a pregnant nigger woman and her baby nigger boy. Second, we will use the same basic principle that we use in breaking a horse, combined with some sustaining factors. What we do with horses is that we break them from one form of life to another; that is we reduce them from one form of life to another; we reduce them from their natural state in nature; whereas nature provides them with the natural capacity to take care of their needs and the needs of their offspring, we break that natural sting of independence from them and thereby create a dependency state so that we may be able to get from them useful production for our business and pleasure.

PRINCIPLES FOR MAKING A NEGRO

Negro means one that has lost the knowledge of himself and is living an unnatural life contrary to his nature. For fear that our future generations may not understand the principles for breaking both horses and men, we lay down the art. For, if we are to sustain our basic economy we must break and tie both of the beasts together. the nigger and the horse. We understand that short range planning in economics results in periodic economic chaos; so that, to avoid turmoil in the economy, it requires us to have breadth

56

and depth in long range comprehensive planning, articulating both skill and sharp perception.

We lay down the following principles for long range comprehensive economic planning.

1.Both horse and nigger are no good to the economy in the wild or natural state.

2.Both must be broken and tied together for orderly production.

3.For orderly futures, special and particular attention must be paid to the female and the young offspring.

4.Both must be crossbred to produce a variety and division of labor.

5.Both must be taught to respond to a peculiar new language.

6.Psychological and physical institutions of containment must be created for both.

We hold the above six cardinal principles as truths to be self-evident based on the following discourse concerning the economics of breaking and tying the horse and nigger together-all inclusive of the six principles laid down above.NOTE: Neither principle alone will suffice for good economics. All principles must be employed for the orderly good of the nation.

According , both a wild horse and a wild or natural nigger is dangerous even if captured, for they will have the tendency to seek their customary freedom, and in so doing might kill you in your sleep. You cannot rest. They sleep while you are awake and are awake while you are asleep.

They are dangerous near the family house and it requires too much labor to watch them from away from the house. Above all you cannot get them to work in this natural state.

Hence, both the horse and the nigger must be broken; that is, break them from one form of mental life to another--keep the body and take the mind. In other words, break the will to resist. Now, the breaking process is the same for both the horse and the nigger, only slightly varying in degrees. But, as we said before, there is an art in long range economic planning. You must keep your eye and thought on the female and the offspring of the horse and the nigger.

A brief discourse in offspring development will shed light on the key to sound economic principles. Pay little attention to the generation of original breaking but concentrate on future generations. THEREFORE IF YOU BREAK THE FEMALE MOTHER, SHE WILL BREAK THE OFFSPRING IN ITS EARLY YEARS OF DEVELOPMENT,and when the offspring is old enough to work, she will deliver it up to you for her normal female protective tendencies will have been lost in the original breaking process.

For example, take the case of the wild stud horse, a female horse and an already infant horse and compare the breaking process with two captured nigger males in their natural state, a pregnant nigger woman with her nigger infant offspring. Take the stud horse, break him for limited containment. Completely break the female horse until she become very gentle whereas you or anyone can ride her in comfort. Breed the mare and the stud until you have the desired offspring. Then you can turn the stud to freedom until you need him again. Train the female horse whereby she will eat out of your hand, and she will in turn, train the infant horses to eat out of your hand also.

When it comes to breaking the uncivilized niggers, use the same process, but vary the degrees and step up the pressure so as to do a complete reversal of the mind. Take the meanest and most restless nigger, strip him of his clothes in front of the remaining male nigger, the female, and the nigger infant, tar and feather him, tie each leg to a different horse faced in different directions, set him afire and beat both horses to pull him apart in front of the remaining nigger. The next step is to take a bull whip and beat the remaining nigger male to the point of death in front of the female and the infant. Don't kill him, but put the fear of God in him, for he can be useful for future breeding.

THE BREAKING PROCESS OF THE BLACK WOMAN!

Then take the female, Run a series of tests on her to see if she will submit to your desires willingly. Test her in every way because she is the most important factor for good economics. If she shows any signs of resistance in submitting completely to your will, do not hesitate to the bull whip on her. Take care not to kill her, for, in doing so, you spoil good economics. When in complete submission, she will train her offspring in the early years to submit to labor when they become of age.

Understanding is the best thing. Therefore we shall go deeper into this area of the subject matter concerning what we have produced here in this breaking process of the female nigger. We have reversed the relationships. In her natural uncivilized state she would have a strong dependency on the uncivilized nigger male, and she would have a limited protective tendency toward her independent male offspring and would raise the female offspring to be dependent like her. Nature had provided for this type of balance. We reversed nature by burning and pulling one uncivilized nigger apart and bull whipping the other to the point of death--all in her presence. By her being left alone, unprotected, with the male image destroyed, the ordeal caused her to move from her psychological dependent state to a frozen independent state.

In this frozen psychological state of independence, she will raise her male and female offspring in reversed roles. For fear of the young male's life, she will psychologically train him to be mentally weak and dependent but physically strong. Because she has become psychologically independent she will train her female offspring to be psychologically independent. What you got? You got the nigger woman out front and the nigger man behind and scared. This is a perfect situation for sound sleep and good economics.Before the breaking process, we had to alertly be on guard at all times.

Now we can sleep soundly, for, out of frozen fear, his woman stands guard for us., He cannot get past her early infant slave molding process. He is a good tool, now ready to be tied to the horse at a tender age. By the time a nigger boy reaches the age of sixteen, he is soundly broken in and is ready for a long life of sound and efficient work and the reproduction of a unit of good labor force. Continually; through the breaking of uncivilized savage niggers, by throwing the nigger female savage into a frozen psychological state of independence, by killing of the protective image, and by creating a submissive dependent mind of the nigger male savage, we have created an orbiting cycle that turns on its own axis forever, unless a phenomenon occurs and re-shifts the positions of the male and the female savages.

Always remember, that the purpose and intent was to create A Slave Consciousness. Now that this has been accomplished, he will do whatever you will him to do because your Mind is his master and his desire is to please you. The time span of sixty-four years (1555 to 1619) has been well spent and should last for centuries until someone comes along and change the Consciousness. Beware of outside influence like their people looking for them or trying to influence their thinking because once the Slave Chain of Thought is broken by a higher power, then our control over the Negro will be lost. As long as they believe that we are God's People the we are secure. In this book, a slave and a Negro are synonymous.

A SPEECH TO AMERICAN SLAVE AND PLANTATION OWNERS IN 1712

Willie Lynch name is best remembered by the term "lynched" , or more expressly put, the hanging of black slaves. Prior to Lynch speech, hanging and other cruel form of punishment were the norm for slave control. Then Lynch spoke this message in America. From that point on, slavery took on new dimensions.

Once this plan was entrenched, it worked disastrously well. The plan is still in motion today. Use this knowledge to overcome the cruel impact of this plan, for the purpose to Unite, rather than to Divide." United We Stand, Divided We Fall."

The Speech

Gentlemen:

I greet you here on the bank of the James River in the year of our Lord one thousand seven hundred an twelve. First, I shall thank you the Gentlemen of the Colony of Virginia for bringing me here.

I am here to help you solve some of your problems with slaves. Your invitation reached me on my modest plantation in the West Indies where I have experimented with some of the newest and still the oldest methods for control of slaves. Ancient Rome would envy us if my program is implemented. As our boat sailed south of the James River, named for our illustrious King, whose version of the Bible we cherish, I saw enough to know that your problem is not unique. While Rome used cords of wood as crosses for standing human bodies along its old highway in great numbers, you are here using the tree and rope on occasion.

I caught the whiff of a dead slave hanging from a tree a couple of miles back. You are not only losing valuable stock by hanging, you are having uprisings, slaves are running away, your crops are sometimes left in the field too long for maximum profit, and you suffer occasional fires. Your animals are killed, Gentlemen you know what your problems are; I do not need to elaborate, I am here to enumerate your problems, I am here to introduce you to a method of solving them.

In my bag here, I have a foolproof method for controlling your Niger slaves. I guarantee every one of you that if installed correctly, it will control the slaves for at least 300 years. My methods are simple and members of your family or overseer can use it.

I have outlined a number of differences among the slaves; and I take these differences and make them bigger. I use fear, distrust, and envy for control purposes. These methods have worked on my modest plantation in the West Indies and it will work throughout the South. Take this simple little list of differences, think about them. On top of my list is "Age" but it is there only because it starts with an "a". The second is color or shade. There is intelligence, size, sex, size of plantation, status of plantation, attitude of owner, whether the slave lives in the valley, on a hill, East, West, North or South, have fine or coarse hair, or is tall or short. Now that you have a list of differences, I shall give you an outline of action but before that I shall assure you that distrust is stronger than trust and envy is stronger than adulation, respect or admiration.

The nigger slave after receiving this indoctrination shall carry on and will become self refueling and self generating for hundreds of years, maybe thousands. Don't forget that you must pitch the old niger slave vs the young niger slave, and the young niger slave against the old niger slave. You must use the light skin slaves vs the dark skin slaves and the dark skin slaves vs the light skin slaves. You must also have your white servants and overseers distrust all niggers but it is necessary that your slaves trust and depend on us. They must Love, Respect, and Trust only us only.

Gentlemen, these kits are our keys to control, use them. Have your wives and children use them, never miss an opportunity. My plan is guaranteed, and the good thing about this plan is that if used intensely for one year , the slaves themselves will remain perpetually distrustful.

Thank you Gentlemen ,
Willie Lynch

CHAPTER VI.

WHITE PEOPLE THINK THAT THEY ARE GOD'S PEOPLE!

SPIRITUAL IDENTITY OF THE BLACKMAN

There are two histories regarding the spiritual identity of the Blackman and the Whiteman. The biblical version gives the identity of the Blackman as the Children of Israel from Noah and his three sons; Shem, Ham, and Japheth. These are the sons of Noah and of them was the whole earth over-spread, Ham is the father of Canaan. Genesis 9:18-19 (All were black people). The generations of Shem begot Abraham, Isaac and Jacob. Jacob's name was changed to Israel (Genesis 32:28) when he prayed for forgiveness for stealing his brother's Birthright. The name Israel means that he prevailed and was converted to a new walk with God. All Black People!

Genesis 35:6 So Jacob came to Luz, which is in the land of Canaan, that is Bethel, he and all his people that were with him. 35:10 and God said unto him thy name is Jacob: thy name shall not be called anymore Jacob, but Israel shall be thy name, and he called his name Israel. Now the sons of Jacob or Israel were twelve; Reuben, Simeon, Levi, Judah, Issachar, Zebulun, Dan, Naph'tali, Gad Asher, Joseph and Benjamin.

Jacob dwelled in the landwhere his father Isaac was in Canaan and built an altar and called the place El Bethel. This is how Israel and his people became famous in scripture because he converted to God and built an altar within the very spot that he ran from his transgression, he not only repented, but dedicated himself and his family to a new way of life. These were your original Jews or Canaanites from Canaan ; ALL BLACK!!

The history of the Children of Israel evolves from this point with Joseph being sold into slavery by his brothers, and being Abraham's Seed would remain in bondage for over 400 years (So-Called Negroes) in a strange land (America), until God would come and set them free (mentally and Spiritually) and bring them out of bondage with great substance. This is the Blackman true Spiritual Identity and it must be understood in order for the Blackman to truly Know Himself. The Whiteman has never been in bondage for 400 years to anyone.

The Whiteman evolved from Europe in the caves and hillsides of that region. Moses brought them out of their misery and taught them Judaism as their Religion. Moses was a Black man and their "Spiritual" father. He led them on to the road of civilization. The Children of Isreal in the Bible and Holy Quran is prophetic and speaks of a future Moses that would lead his people out of mental, spiritual and physical bondage of 400 years, that takes place in America.

White people claim to be the Children of Israel and the Seed of Abraham was denied by Jesus, when he explained to them (Jews) that their father was the Devil, a liar from the beginning, and as a result of being a liar, he was cast out of Heaven and into the wilderness for 2,000 years. Wherein Moses came to them and raised them up. He

67

became their leader, savior, and God. On accepting the Faith (Judaism) they became Abraham's Seed by "Faith" and not by Nature. By accepting Abraham's religion by Faith does not make them Abraham's people by Nature. Jesus set the record straight about their ancestry, and they tried to kill him by crucifixion. Again, the original Children of Israel by Nature are black people, and the Children of Israel by Faith are White people.

CHILDREN OF ISRAEL IN AMERICA!

Matthew 24-28 Where the carcass is there will be eagles gathered together . The symbol of the United States of America is the Eagle, and the symbol of a dead nation it a carcass. The so-called Negroes have been in America for over 400 years as slaves until they have become completely dead to the knowledge of who they are and God must come to fulfill the scripture and rescue and resurrect this dead carcass or nation of people.

As a result of 400 years of mis-treatment and brainwashing concerning his identity, the Blackman is fearful about leaving the Whiteman and doing something for himself. He has been forced to call himself a Negro, accept a history that is not his own, taught false concepts about God in Christianity, and he has no economic base to start doing for self. Discrimination, lack of job opportunity, culture, and just coming out of physical slavery has left the Blackman and Woman a mental cripple.

When God comes, his first duty will be raise up a Moses to fulfill the real scripture of the real Children of Israel (So Called Negroes) out of Pharaoh's Government and lifestyle which is America. The purpose and intent of Moses is to re-educate the Children of Israel into the method of building a nation for themselves within America, with their own values, economics, and way of life called Islam. God is calling for a mental and spiritual separation and not a land or geographical separation, because the earth belong to the Blackman. In order to do this, God has provided a plan in scripture that will lead the So Called Negroes out of bondage and on to the Promise Land.

1. Moses first problem will be Disbelief. So-Called Negroes do not believe that they should have their own nation.
2. God must punish Pharaoh (America) with plagues like food droughts, fire, hail, storms, and water and death to bring about a separation between the two nations.
3. Once separated, and in the desert, or on their own psychologically, Moses can start dispensing the laws that the nation would live by.
4. Stages of Growth for the nation; Backbiting, moaning, regret, and longing to be with their slave-master for over 435 years.
5. Moses established the Law for over 40 years until a new generation was born to see the Promise Land.
6. The Seed of the Original Children of Israel or Abraham's Seed will go on to build A new nation.

Children of Israel

To summarize this story, The time has come in scripture for a mental, spiritual, and economical, and psychological separation. The hold-up is that the Blackman and woman (ex-slaves physically) do not want to separate because they are in love with white people. So God must send plagues in the form of economic disasters, unemployment, crimes, drugs, murder, and Aids. These plagues will force the Blackman and woman to seek refuge in God's Laws for his salvation. Once the separation take place the Negroes will grumble and backslide until they develop Faith in God and his Divine Guidance.

This will not take place until much suffering and the manifestation of God's power. After this period, the Blackman will be born with a new spirit of nationhood, and this new spirit will give birth to the Black Nation in America. In order for a nation to be born, the first people must give birth to a new generation that will bring this idea of nationhood into fruition. God has put it into the hearts and minds of the Blackman and woman of America to have a nation that they can call their own, and this will come into being.

What God is doing now is removing the obstruction that has been keeping the Blackman from Doing for Self. This obstruction could be the Whiteman or a Negro that hates himself and kind; whatever it is it must go ! The real Promise Land is Mental and Spiritual and being able to live in God's world of Peace and enjoying the fruits of your labor. Not living in a world of murder, crime and peace-breakers. It is time for the Children of Israel to form their own government and start fulfilling their destiny as written in scripture.

SATAN'S TIME TO RULE IS UP!

The six-thousand years of Satan to rule over the earth was up in 1914, and it was the beginning of World War I, WW II, and WW III will complete the downfall of Satan and the beginning of God's world of peace and prosperity. This period that we are living in (1995) is a Grace Period or transitional period of slowly bringing down a world power. As we witness this change in ruling powers or change in governments, the Blackman will gradually be resurrected back to his rightful position of world power. He will regain some authority in his homeland. Regain his governments, and just as it was prophesied of the Whiteman in Genesis 1:26 , Let Us Make Man , and let him have dominion over the fish of the sea, and over the fowl of the air, and over everything that creepeth. The process will be reversed and the Blackman will once again be in control of his destiny.

The seventh day (seven thousand years) is the day of rest for the Devil or Satan to rule over the earth. The seventh day is the Day of Reality between God and the Devil. This is the Day of Manifestation in which everything is made known to Man so that he can make a decision as to who he will serve as God of his life. The seventh day is the day that God makes known the identity of the Devil to the world. God promised Cain that his identity would be concealed and he would be respite until that day .

Satan's Time Is Up!

The seventh day is the day that Allah makes himself known to the world, and it is a great day for some and a dreadful day for others. The seventh day began in 1914 and was officially announced by God in Person, the Supreme Being, the long awaited Messiah of the Christians, and the Mahdi of the Muslims in the person of Master Fard Muhammad. His first revelation was that the Whiteman was the Devil and the root cause of all the world's problems. The Blackman has been made a slave to the Whiteman the world over, and he must be freed mentally and spiritually and restored to his rightful place as God of the earth. This process of Resurrection is taking place gradually.

In the seventh thousand year, all types of slavery thinking must be abolished, and the people must learn to think like a God. The people must have "A New Way Of Thinking "! Jesus said in Matthew 21:43 The Kingdom of God shall be taken from you and given to another, bringing forth the fruits of it. The Blackman of America will be given a new nation, that nation will be Spiritual in nature and in it's conceptual viewpoint of life. The current world view of life is economics first, and forget God and his Laws.

However, in order for the Negroes to accept the Kingdom of God, and maintain the Laws of God, they must be re-made mentally in their thinking and given a new perspective of God and his Kingdom. The Negroes have been mis-educated, poisoned, and led in the wrong direction by the Jews, Christians, and other religious leaders when it comes to the true knowledge of God. They are not prepared to rule themselves or any other nation . If they had their own nation today, it could be stolen from them the same way the first nation was stolen, through tricks, lies, and deception. They must learn the Mental Keys to unlocking a person's mind and seeing what is there, the mental wisdom to maneuver in a world of international danger, and the mental keys to identifying the nature of people.

The purpose of the Resurrection of the Dead is to put this Divine understanding in to the heads of the so-called Negroes or Blackman of America. This Divine insight, Knowledge, Wisdom will unlock their dead minds and give them the tools necessary to build a nation. The Seventh Day is the Preparation Day, the Resurrection Day, the Acceptance Day of the nation that is given to them from God. This is the Day of Lazarus (Blackman) being raised from the Dead. Jesus plainly states that Lazarus was not dead but only asleep, and he must go awake him from his sleep. Master Fard Muhammad is that Jesus that is waking the Blackman up from 400 years of mental sleep, the Bible describes it as four days.

In order for Lazarus to be resurrected, he must be believe in God (The teachings of Master Fard Muhammad) and he will find life to get up and build. The true meaning of Life after Death is that it is a stage in evolution. Just as from dust is evolved the Physical Man, so it is that from his deeds is evolved the higher Spiritual Man. The purpose of the Resurrection is to evolve the higher Spiritual Man of God. Just as the small life germ grows up to become the man, and he does not lose his individuality, although he undergoes many changes, so it is that the Man of God goes

73

through many changes in attributes, and grow into that which the person could never conceive of.

When a Man of God raises a person from the dead, it is the evolving of this individual through many stages of higher development to spiritual perfection. THIS IS THE MEANING OF JESUS RAISING LAZARUS FROM THE DEAD! When this same principle of evolution is applied to the so-called Negroes of America, one can see them Rising from a dead state of Mind or from their Grave of Ignorance about Self, God, and the Devil. The Hereafter is not a mystery that begins after physical death or beyond the grave, but rather it begins here in this life, on this good earth. It means to be here alive after you have stop living your life like a devil and caused yourself to be dead and have no spirit concerning God. Thus, God comes into your life and re-energizes you with his spirit and causes you to live again as a born-again Child of his Kingdom, YOU ARE NOW IN THE HEREAFTER.

The reason it is so difficult for some people to believe the true meaning of the Hereafter or the Resurrection is because they have lived such a miserable life that they can't believe that there is nothing else, so it helps them psychologically to hold on to this fantasy or mystery thinking. But life can be very beautiful if you are Righteous. America is a Slave-Making nation, although its image is something different. A nation's image is how it represents itself to the rest of the world. America presents itself as a benefactor , a great business nation, a peace loving nation, and friendly nation to other in distress.

The truth is that the Blackman and Woman of America is still in bondage with white-people Names from slavery. No Money or Reparation from 400 years of labor, Alcohol, Drugs and other vices are kept in the black communities to keep the slaves (Black People) pacified.

The cause of the problem is within the Whiteman's psyche and manifested in the Blackman 's environment. The image of the Blackman is that of a slave tied to the umbilical cord (Mind of whiteman) for survival. The Blackman (slave) does not have an accurate image of himself and must be totally re-educated into the knowledge of himself. Image-wise the Blackman is a reverse whiteman with a different color. A man or nation is only a man or nation when it is operating from their own God Given -Image.

The reason the Whiteman is still to blame for the condition of the Blackman is because he still will not Admit the fact of What He Has Done To the Blackman Culturally, Historically, Psychologically, Economically, and Morally. Until something is done to address these issues then he is still a hypocrite and Affirmative Action and other programs are only "window-dressing to his continued slave-making tactics." The Blackman of America must establish ties with his African brothers in the East to be culturally, economically, and spiritually committed to being free

LOST AND FOUND PEOPLE OF GOD

The Blackman of America has been lost from his African and Asian brothers for over 400 years and it took God in the person of Master Fard Muhammad to find them and re-acquaint them with their brothers and sisters in the East. Read about the Prodigal Son and the Lost Sheep returned to the fold. The solution to this re-union is that the Blackman must re-establish some relationships in Economics to become closer as brothers. Re-establish religious ties with the same God, and the same values. In order to help the Blackman in his transition to self-rule, he has been given Islam as a Way of Life.

This new Way of Life will change the Blackman conception of himself, his values towards others, his knowledge of God and the Devil , and put him in position to receive the favors of God in this last days of Satan's civilization. A famine is coming upon America and the Blackman and woman must be prepared or suffer the consequences. This famine is written up under the story of Joseph in the land of Egypt. Joseph (blackman) must practice safe economical principles before the famine in order for him to be ready during the famine. The prescription is : Appoint black officer in major area throughout the country to collect money (Charity) to buy the harvest (crops) of each year to be stored in the cities for future use, and to buy other things that can be use during a crisis. A wise man prepares for the future while the fool sits idle and laughs.

The so-called Negroes is being used by God as a test of Faith. If he pass the test, he can save many people from the destruction of famine, and become a blessing to the world . God's intention is that the Negroes become Black in Name, Spirit, and in Deeds to lead the other nations to Righteousness. The Blackman of America has lived under the rule and control of the Devil for over four hundred years. His Mind has been taken away and given a Negro's Mind (Dead Mind). He was given poison food to eat (hog), poison drink (alcohol), false religion (Christianity) which is a perfect religion for making black slaves because it shows all the prophets as white and black people as slaves, which is ordained by God. Christianity is the Devil's religion.

After the Blackman culture was stripped from him, he did not know Who He Was or Where He Came From, and all of these things were prophesied to happen until the coming of God , after Satan's time was up to rule. Genesis 15: 14-15 And also that nation, whom they shall serve, will I judge: and afterward they shall come out with great substance. And thou shall go to their fathers in peace; thou shall be buried in a good old age. Two-thirds of the scripture has been fulfilled; Satan's time was up in 1914 and we can see that he is trying Integration to keep his slave close to him. The Nation of Islam has been established to build a New House for the Blackman survival, and Divine Guidance from God is its foundation.

Lost and Found

The foundation of the Nation is God (master Fard Muhammad is the personification of God like Jesus, Moses, or Abraham) the Messenger is the Hon. Elijah Muhammad, who established the truth among the Negroes like Prophet Muhammad of 1400 years ago did among the Arabs. Finally, the Bible and Holy Quran are our books of reference to our history but must be interpreted with Divine Guidance through our leader Hon. Elijah Muhammad or the nation will fall victim to the Devil's interpretation.

The Bible and Holy Quran are books that use symbols, parables, and allegorical statements to describe people, places and things. These books describe the times, trials and tribulations of God's people (Righteous), also, heaven and hell, and the reward and punishment of God's people as told by Prophets. The original people of scripture were black and not white. The Whiteman stole the scriptural identity of black people by substituting themselves in the place of the original black people as the people of God. The Whiteman was able to do this because God gave them dominion over everything on the earth for a period of time; Six Thousand Years. The seventh day, he must rest; his rule over the people of earth must come to an end. Then God would come and teach the world of the complete truth of what has transpired during the last six-thousand years. The Whiteman's day of rest began in Nineteen Fourteen 1914 AD.

This is why this truth is being preached all over the world especially the United States because it is time for the Blackman to Wake Up!

It is Time for him to re-build his nation! Re-build here in America ! The so-called Negroes have been captured, made slaves, and scattered all over the United States, like the dried bones in the valley in Ezekiel vision. The Negroes have become like dried bones to the point wherein the prophets are wondering "Can these bones live?"

This is the condition of the Blackman and woman of America, however, the Son of Man in the person of Master Fard Muhammad has said to the Blackman "Behold , O my People, I will open your graves, and cause you to come out of your graves, and bring you into the land of Israel. And ye shall know that I am the Lord, when I have opened your graves, O my people, and brought you up out of your graves, and put my spirit in you, and ye shall live, and I shall place you in your own land; then shall you know that I, the Lord, have spoken it, and performed it, saith the Lord.

Once the Negroes are separated mentally and spiritually, Gog and Magog will attack them and try to bring them back into the mainstream of American thought. This attack will cause their ultimate destruction. The Holy Quran gives the identity of Gog and Magog on page 591, Chapter 18, footnote 1525 as the ancestors of the Slav and Teutonic Races of Eastern Europe. It is clear that Gog and Magog are God's enemies because they attack Israel (So Called Negroes), and that they are the European People or White People. The So Called Negroes were stripped of their Culture, History, Religion, Names, Economy, God, and Dignity as a people in America, and this is the same place where God is going to re-build the nation once again !

Lost and Found

The vision of Ezekiel dry bones coming together is how it will take place. The bones (So Called Negroes) will hear the word of God because God will blow his breath (New Spiritual Teachings) and they will live. God will put new sinew and flesh on them (new strength and vitality) and once they began to get strong in God's ways and less in the Devil's ways, there will be a great shaking, and then all of a sudden the dry bones will come together. Once the Word of God is accepted by the So Called Negroes and lived spiritually, then they are going to stand up on their feet, like a great army in America!

Don't forget that Joseph became a ruler in the land where he was a slave! This is the destiny of the Blackman and Woman, and any one tampering with this mission of God of Resurrecting this Dead Nation will be in danger of being destroyed, because this is God's Mission. Mental Chastisement is one of the ways that God uses to punish a person or nation that interferes with a Divine Mission; he causes the person to go insane so that his work can be complete.

For example, four thousand years ago, when white people were disobeying God's laws in the Holy Land, and were exiled to Europe where they went insane and lived the life of animals , just like a beast in the field. He is commonly referred to as the Caveman, and this is a result of interfering with God's people and their way of life. The same thing happened to King Nebuchadnezzar (king of Babylon) who thought that he was God, and he went insane and was driven from men, ate grass like an oxen, his hair grown out like eagle feathers and his nails like bird claws. This parable from Daniel 4:33 clearly indicates that the Whiteman and King Nebuchadnezzar are one and the same.

CHAPTER VII.

AFROCENTRICITY IN AMERICA

Afrocentricity is a term used in the black community to indicate that the nerve center for thinking and the origin of black people is in Africa. It is applied in the school-system to suggest that blacks should be taught an Afrocentric curriculum instead of an exclusive Eurocentric curriculum or Negro History. The term Negro must be removed from the books because it is the same as Nigger and is offensive to blacks. However, the basis of education is Mind development, and if the minds of Blacks in America is to be developed properly it must include all of their history, including Negro or Nigger history. Just as the Jews say "Never Forget The Holocaust" Blacks should never forget their Holocaust In America" It is a part of History. All history is not pleasant, but it must be accepted as part of the evolution of a people.

Afrocentric education teaches the Blackman a knowledge of himself that goes back beyond the cotton fields and into the palaces of Egypt. It gives a knowledge of the Black Kings and Queens that ruled the world hen the whiteman was eating bugs out of the ground for lunch.

Eurocentricity is a term that has its origin in Europe and its philosophy is that the Whiteman is superior to other men on earth, and that the nerve center for thought begins in Europe. This has already been explained from the beginning of the book, wherein the Whiteman was given six-thousand years to rule the earth with violence, wisdom, tricks, and any means necessary to fulfill scripture of "Let

Us Make A New Man and Give Him dominion over the earth for six days; then God would come in the last days, and then he must rest. The authority to rule the world was given to him by the Blackman , and it was the Blackman who kept him in power all during his tenure on earth by sending him prophets to instruct him along the way. Moses was sent to him, Jesus was sent, and the Blackman of America helped set him on top of the world.

The reason for his success is that God has ordained it Divinely in order for the Righteous or Blackman to "See" what was in his own nature (evil tendencies) and a specimen must be brought out of the Blackman; he must live under this wicked specimen, in order to "See" that Righteousness is the only way for the people of God to live and this experiment will never be done again. THE WHITEMAN AND HIS WORLD IS AN EXPERIMENT IN LIVING A LIFE OF UNRIGHTEOUSNESS; THE DETRIMENT OR BENEFIT OF SUCH A LIFE. The conclusion is in and the entire population of earth is 100% Dis-satisfied with this evil way of life, and they want it removed immediately!

There is no question that an Afrocentric way of life with Sociology, Psychology, Religion (Islam), Economics, Culture, Morals, and the complete knowledge of Self must be re-introduced to black students in school and the black community at large before their will ever be any peace between the Races. These God-given principles of development are vital for any nation to rise, but it is clear that a people who stripped you of your humanity, mis-treat you constantly will not Teach you of yourself, regardless of what name that you call it.

It is time to give the Whiteman back his Name, Culture, Way of Life, and Evil Habits then Afrocentricity.

RE-BUILDING THE BLACK COMMUNITY

The essence of re-building the black nation in America has to be spiritual in nature in order to address the moral decay within the black community. Secondly, the economic aspect must be dealt with from a national black perspective instead of a local viewpoint. Black people must set aside some form of taxation or donations to rebuild their communities. The Federal government is not going to do it for you. There must be a mental awareness that will enable blacks to see that this is their own responsiblity and not white folks. Each community must police it's own front and backyard. Drug dealers must become national priority wherein other blacks can come in if necessary to weed out the undesirables. Programs must be established to address that need.

Once the Blackman is separated mentally and understand his responsibility, then the whiteman might assist you, but not until you accept your responsibility . When the Whiteman was being made through a process called Restrictive Marrying or marrying the lighter onto the lighter until you have white, or unlike black. There were no prisons for criminals that broke the law because all who were found breaking the law were executed. If you were unable to produce children in one year after marriage, then you were executed because you were considered no good for building a nation.

The Point Is: In building or re-building a nation there is no time to waste on people that are law-breakers, deviants, or anyone that is not 100% behind the efforts of nation-building. We Are 400 years behind Now!

The economics of re-building is simple because everyone must pay their taxes to build the nation. It is paid the same way as income taxes are paid to the American Government. The only difference is that this money is used to Re-build the Black Communities Throughout America. The same law would apply to people stealing our money for Re-building. "Off Go Their Heads" This might seem extreme but think of the damage done to our people, so this would be considered Treason, and Treason is an offense punishable by death.

First of all, God must give us the Law or Authority to execute punishment on our people like the Children of Israel had once they were in the desert. We will never have the authority to punish our people for their crimes as long as will are subject to American or the Devil's Jurisprudence. He loves crimes so why should he punish offenders. In Islam there are Laws that are called the Rested Laws of Islam and if carried into practice they will clean up our communities without bloodshed. These are the Restricted Laws!

1. Obey Allah, his Apostle, and believe in the message sent to you.
2. Obedience to his Apostle is obedience to Allah.
3. Workshop no God but Allah.
4. Fear no one but Allah

5. Obey those in authority among you, and obey non-believers in authority over you as long as it does not conflict with your religion.
6. No drinking (Wine, beer, Whiskey, ale, Alcohol, or other intoxicants).
7. It is forbidden to commit fornication or adultery.
8. It is forbidden to eat the pig or its by-products.
9. No insubordination, slack talk, or gossip.
10. Do not lust.
11. Do Not associate with those in bad standings (within community).
12. No gambling of any kind (Numbers, dice, cards, games of chance).
13. No smoking of any kind (Reefers or cigarettes, cigar or pipe).
14. No Dope (Heroin, cocaine, or any kind of dope or drugs).
15. No Lying (Speak the truth regardless of circumstances).
16. No Stealing
17. Do not deal with hypocrites or show sympathy to them.
18. Do not commit acts of violence on other or unto yourself).
19. Do unto others as you would have others do unto you.
20. Must be clean at all times (Mind and Body).

These Restricted Laws are from God Almighty and any community can prosper if they are practiced. Moses was given Laws to clean up the Children of Israel. These are tailor-made to remedy our current ills and afflictions for Re-building the Black Community.

Once the Laws are established within the new black community, an economic blueprint for growth must be developed. A nation's money must be spent to protect the people and it is difficult to plan for black people because they do not trust their own people. This lack of trust is what the Blackman must be re-educated spiritually , in order to open his eyes to the times and what must be done. The Children of Israel were the same way, they trusted Pharaoh but they did not trust their own people with their money. The economy of the United States is struggling to keep from collapsing from so much debt but blacks still trust them. The Day of Financial Reckoning is coming, a wise man will seek another foundation to build on.

Black So Called Americans are the first fired after being the last hired, Discrimination Laws are passed each year, and Laws on Affirmative Action are being repealed. The leadership (black) should form a board of political, religious, banking, industry and every phase of society to create a National Banking System. Money can be deposited from around the world to help resurrect the Blackman of America. This money can be re-invested back into the building of the nation. Farms must be bought to feed the hungry. Hospitals must be built to aid the sick and destitute. Houses must be built to shelter the homeless. Banking can create wealth in the black community. This may seem impossible but it can be done!

The problem is having Faith in the Black Leadership to get the job done, and the leadership must come together to formulate the plans and present them to the Black Community in America. The Nation of Islam under the leadership of Hon. Elijah Muhammad and his followers are working on uniting the Black Community to accomplish this worthy goal. The Hon. Elijah Muhammad stated: No nation can be free (Black or White) that does not control its own Economics. The Blackman of America does not have a system in place to Save, Spend, or Control his money in such a manner that it comes back to his community to support his community.

The Blackman money supports every body's community but his own. As a result, his community is run-down, second -rate, there are no black owned hospital, grocery chains, gas and oil companies, or any concerns that produce the essential of life like food, clothing and shelter. The Resurrection of The Dead Blackman is first Spiritual because he must Wake Up to God Within Himself before he can progress. Second, it is a Mental endeavor that must be Thought-Out and Planned from poverty to wealth as a nation, and not just as individual blacks. This Plan for economic progress as a nation will free the nation and make us recognized as equals the world over.

God is giving us a plan to put in place "A National Banking System" to use our money for our own needs and services. Black People have Billions of Dollars just lying in the Whiteman banks doing not for themselves, but in reality is working against blacks in the form of Racist Policies against minorities.

Blacks spend over Four Billion Dollars a Year, and none of it comes back into the Black Community because THERE IS NO BLACK COMMUN ITY organized to do anything with the money. If a famine or hard times comes upon America (Like the Depression of 1929), everyone must eat, and God always provides the means for his people to eat. God does not make them suffer because he shifts the power. The Blackman of America is powerless in terms of Economics because he has no National Banking System in place to provide for his needs in an International Crisis. That is the main problem! He has billions flowing through his hands every year, but he has no Banking System to retain it for himself. The National Banking System will eliminate a four-hundred year old problem--which is No Black Economic Control Of His Resources.

This economic problem is rooted in another problem --which is A Poor Self Image about Self and a Positive self-image about White. The Blackman feels more secure with his money in the Whiteman's banks than in his own banks, What A Pitiful Slave!! An Image is the physical, mental, or spiritual reproduction of something or someone. The Negro is a spiritual and mental reproduction of the Whiteman. The Whiteman gave the blackman guidelines on how to be a slave. He taught him every mental and spiritual concept about slavery and his duties. He taught him to worship him as God in Christianity. He taught him to eat swine, which sounds 1/16 of the mental capacities. He taught him a false history of himself, and he taught him to look to him for life-long guidance.

National Banking System

What the Blackman accepted from the Whiteman in slavery was A New Identity! This new identity is what the Blackman is today, A Modern Day Slave with the whiteman's name, Culture, Religion, and the time frame for this was from 1555 to 1619., and the reason that the Whiteman wants to take away that sixty-four years is because it to make the world think that blacks came here as Negroes in Jamestown, Va. Wherein the truth is that it took these sixty-four years of killing, poisoning, and training the minds of black babies to become perfect slaves. From that point on, a new existence of slaves (Called Negroes) was born here in America.

They had no image or conception of where they came from, or where they were going in life, (some still don't today). The original black people that arrived on the Good Ship Jesus were allowed to propagate and have babies, because it was the babies that were made slaves and not the original people (Re-read chapter six and see how they were treated). The Whiteman raised them the way he wanted to. Their minds were trained to Love, Care, Grieve, and Work for White people. On the other hand, they were taught to Mistrust, Back-bite, Hate, Fight, and Kill one another. This condition is still prevalent and it is the main reason that blacks cannot organize and build A National Banking System. Remember this, the Blackman has accepted mentally and spiritually this new" Identity of Negro" that the Whiteman has given him in slavery.

THE BLACKMAN AND WOMAN MUST BE "BORN-AGAIN".

Who are the so-called American Negroes, Colored People, or African Americans . Let us study history and find out. The Cradle of Civilization for the Blackman is the African or Asian Continent. The Cradle of Civilization for the Whiteman is Europe. The first known societies or civilizations that were developed by Man was along the Tigris, Euphrates, and Nile Valleys, and they were developed by the Blackman. All of the Prophets such as Moses, Jesus, David, Solomon, and Muhammad came from this region of the world and were sent to Europe to try and convert the Europeans (White people) to Righteousness or civilized behavior, and they were rejected.

All of the sciences from mathematics, Numerical system, Biology, and Medicine were transported from the East and given to the Europeans to build up their civilization. The European philosophers i.e. Socrates,Plato, and Aristotle received their wisdom from the Blackman of the East. They used this knowledge to establish their educational system on the concept of: Know Thyself. They set-up their political system on the concept of the city-state .The Europeans used to marvel at the Blackman's way of life such as In-door baths, and toilets, A sewage system, paved streets, public lights, parks, hospitals, schools and universities. This is all reflected in your history books but not in the whiteman history books.

Born Again

The Whiteman portrays this as his world, but it is not true, he was in Europe living like a savage, trying to learn about life and its true meaning. Everything that the Europeans have today is a result of the Blackman sharing his wisdom. When the Europeans came to power in the last thousand years of their existence, and their Language became universal, they incorporated the word Negro into their vocabulary as meaning Black, because they associated blacks as living along the Niger River.

The Blackman has never referred to himself as a Negro, that started with the Whiteman. The Blackman has always been named according to his homeland, Nationality or his Religion. Negro does not refer to any of these, in fact, the word Negro means Dead. Spiritually speaking, the term Nigger is a characteristic of a stingy, greedy or thankless person and Negro is an extension of that character. So, a characteristic cannot be a people's heritage, origin, or name-sake. The correct meaning of the word Negro is :A person or nation that has lost the knowledge of themselves and is living their life like a beast or a savage-minded person. It is a State of Mind and Not A Color!

So, since the term Negro is A State of Mind, this means that the Blackman must be "Born Again" into a new state of mind or "consciousness" of his true self. He must become conscious again of his greatness as a people. The Blackman was the first Artist, and I don't mean in the Caves of Europe; I mean that he drew pictures on the earth that cannot be viewed until you are miles above the earth. He has some of the oldest artifacts and drawings known.

The drawings are on rocks, basalt, bones, and Ivory. This is the true history of the Blackman (So Called Negroes), and not Greco-Roman or European history.

BORN AGAIN IN RELIGION

The Blackman is the father and architect of religion. The oldest and most notable statue in the world bears the face of a Blackman (Sphinx).. It was erected about five-thousand years ago BC. , all of the ancient God had broad noses, woolly hair, and were black. In the Bible Daniel 7:9 God is described as having hair as pure wool. The Bible originated in ancient Egypt, where according to Aristotle and Herodotus, the population was all black.

The Psalms were written by Pharaoh Akhenaton; The Ethiopians gave the idea of Right and Wrong and thus laid the foundation for Religion of any kind. In fact, all of the ancient worthies that wrote scripture (Solomon, Daniel, David , Moses were all black) including the prophets that delivered the scripture to different people at different times. The social and moral heritage that the Hebrew received from Moses came from the Egyptians. All white people ever did was receive, read, and reject scriptures!

Jesus was a half-original man , a prophet, that was sent to white people in Europe to help further the teachings of Moses on how to live a Righteous life, but he failed in his mission. The quality of Righteousness is not in them. Prophet Muhammad came six-hundred years after him and was inspired with the Holy Quran as a revelation of the last days of these people and their identity. Also, he saw the prophecy of black people been lost from their own kind for four hundred years in another religion, believing in another prophet as God, and they must be raised up in the Right Religion in the Right State of Mind.

Being raised in another religion (Christianity) is really what killed the Blackman Spiritually to the Knowledge of himself and God. HE MUST RETURN TO HIS OWN RELIGION! Christianity is the Whiteman's conception of religion; He does not understand religion because he will not practice what he say he believes in. He uses religion to tie up peoples Mind in a false lifestyle to himself. He is the God of Christianity and not Jesus. Black people are religious by nature, but to prosper, they must be in the right religion to get the right results. Hitler was a Christian, Stalin was a Christian, Jim Jones was a Christian, Truman was a Christian, and they all slaughtered many people in the name of Jesus. The house of Christianity is falling down because it is built on lies and false concepts about God.

Blackman, come to your religion and God (Islam and Allah), and see the truth of Who is God and Who is the Devil, there is no mystery in Islam, because when you know God and the Devil, the mystery is removed. There is no life after physical death, there is no heaven in the sky, there is no angels flying around with wings singing songs. There are no gold streets where you can walk around shouting all day and drinking milk and honey.

Those were pacifiers and parables that were taught to the slaves in physical slavery to keep them content to wait on there reward after they die.

BORN AGAIN IN CULTURE

Culture is the socially transmitted behavioral patterns of a people's beliefs, institutions, arts, works, and thoughts. A people's culture become its way of life or habitual manner of living. After being made slave in America. The Blackman made a culture for himself in order to exist. This culture became known as Negro History or the Negro Experience. This culture has its own way of life, dietary laws, belief system, institutions, and society. This culture existed for three hundred and ten years during slavery and was perpetuated by the whiteman. It is still in existence today and is still sponsored by the Whiteman through such organizations as United Negro College Fund, NAACP, and the Black Church.

These three groups or organization do more to keep the Negro Culture alive and well than the Whiteman himself, and the sad fact is that it is a dying culture based on falsehood , lies and inferiority. It Is Time To Be Born Again In Another Culture that represents the true Name, dignity, and Self-Worth of our people. The Name Negro must go because that State of Mind is leaving black people as we come to know ourselves. It is time to give up the old Negro Culture and reclaim your own way of life.

Born Again

Your own way of life is Righteousness, and it is called Islam today because Islam is a Righteous Way of Life, and second, it did not comes from White people but it came from God and our own culture of old. This culture operates according to Law and not Lawlessness. I Islam there is no lying, cheating, and Born Again in Culture stealing from your brothers and sisters. There are no sex-theaters in this culture. No prostitution of any kind. This is why the Whiteman, Lucifer, the Devil was kicked out of heaven (Black society in Middle East) and over into Hell (Hills and Caves of Europe) for breaking the laws of the Blackman's culture and society. This is also why a Negro's Culture will not survive because it is a product of the Whiteman and his society. The habits of the Negroes are the same as the Whiteman. There must be a Re-birth in the Consciousness of the Blackman for Righteousness.

Once the Whiteman was in Europe, he established his own society of filth that has engulfed the whole earth. The so-called Negroes became a part of it when they were kidnapped, brought to America and made slaves. God warns the Negroes to come out of her in scripture in these words: Exodus 6 5-7 And I have also heard the groaning of the Children of Israel, I am the Lord, and I will bring you out from under the burdens of the Egyptians (Americans) , and I will rid you of their bondage, and I will redeem you with an out stretched arm, and with great judgments; and I will be to you a God: and ye shall know that I am the Lord your God, who bring you out from under the burden of the Egyptians (Americans).

These scriptures clearly shows that the culture of the Negroes was one of slavery and that God will come to remove that condition mentally, spiritually, psychologically, and economically by bringing to the Blackman his own culture and way of life. Some Black people have become so accustomed to slavery as a way of life that they do not want to change and accept God's way of life. All those Negroes that feel this way will not live on in history through their prodigy, because slavery is over, and the foundation is being removed every day. God has fulfilled his covenant with the Blackman and anyone that does not want their own culture (Islam), will go down with the Devil in his culture. The time for the Whiteman culture to thrive is over, it has seen its best years, It is on its way down, So hurry onto your own culture and live.

There are many cultures on earth that the so-called Negroes could adapt and be raised up in a civilized manner. However, God, in the person of Master Fard Muhammad has chosen Islam for the Negroes because it completes his favor on the Blackman and makes him perfect, or he continues to strive for perfection. Islam has no mystery or spooks in it. Everything in life can be explained including the origin of God and the Devil. Islam is Peace. Islam teaches its members to have money, good homes, friend, knowledge, wisdom and understanding, and to live a highly civilized life, and not a savage life.

The Negroes have lived a life like unto a savage or beast in the field for four-hundred years, and now it is time for a new culture and way of life (Islam).

Born Again

Islam is a voluntary society and no one is forced to be a Muslim. (A Muslim is one who submits to do the will of God). Once the Blackman accepts Islam and start to build his own culture and community with his own people, there is no limit to the progress and advancement that he can make in his own Culture.

BORN AGAIN IN ECONOMICS

Economics is the management of the resources, i.e. labor, money or resources of the nation. The Blackman of America has no economy to manage his resources that are lying dormant in the Whiteman banks. As a result of this lack of an economic system that he can call his own, he is an economic slave to the whiteman, although he has resources. The Blackman spends billions of dollars a year but has no voice as to how his money is spent within his own community. He cannot even demand a loan to beautify his community with his own money. Millions of blacks are on welfare, no jobs, ghetto housing, poor medical care, and all this is due to Fear of The Whiteman, and not standing up and demand some type of control of your money through his economic system.

There are no museum to depict our correct history. No black owned and operated hospitals or Aid Stations in the inner cities for emergencies.

98

No supermarket chains around the country selling black goods and services. No ships on the seas carryings our goods to other ports. No trucks on the highways delivering and exchanging our products. These things can be done if the Blackman controlled the money that he already has in the banks of the Whiteman by establishing his own economic network. WHERE ARE ALL OF THOSE PREACHERS WHEN YOU NEED ONE, TO TEACH ON THIS TRUTH!

White people says that there is no need for a black economy, but try and tell that to the Chinese, Arabs, or Indians. These people are getting rich with there own communities by managing their own money in there own economic structure or system. The Blackman is still a slave to the whiteman mentally and he does not want to do anything that will disturb the master. The whiteman controls the blackman through his Economic System in slavery and he controls him today through the economic system.

The Whiteman has been controlling the economics of the Blackman ever since he has been in America. But God wants to establish a separate economic base under his leadership. When the Blackman realizes that his economic base is in jeopardy with the Whiteman (Crash of 1929) he will hurry and start building for himself, if he intends to survive the coming world economic crash.

BORN AGAIN IN GOD'S NAMES

Negroes do not have their own Names because White people stripped them of their names in slavery and still have not given them back. Blacks are still using white peoples names as their own today , 130 years after slavery ended legally. Negroes have been using White people Names for so long that they have lost the knowledge of how valuable it is to have your own name. McDuffy, Smitz, or Bush are European names, but Muhammad, Sharrief, and Mubara are the names that blacks had before coming here to be made slaves in America.

Names symbolizes our culture and habit of thought and it is obvious that blacks still Think like white people. God wants to change all that by giving you one of his hundred names so that you can be identified as one of his children (Change Your Slave Name To A Name Of God)!

PART III.

GOD COMES TO MAKE THE BLACKMAN IN HIS IMAGE!

SEPARATION IS THE KEY
MENTAL AND SPIRITUAL SEPARATION!

Hon. Elijah Muhammad discusses with Martin Luther King that Separation and not Integration is the key to Black peop Building and Doing for Self in America.

CHAPTER VIII.
THE BIRTH OF A NATION
(Master Fard Muhammad)

Master Fard Muhammad, or the Second Jesus is our Savior and Deliverer from the evils of this Whiteman's world . This man is giving us the knowledge, wisdom, and understanding to see the conditions of despair and do something about it. His wisdom breaks the shackles that bound the mind and hearts of the So Called Negroes. He is the best friend that the Blackman has ever had because he ask for nothing and gives us his all. He is referred to as the Good Samaritan in the Bible that befriends a stranger who had fallen victim to a robber and a thief (sounds familiar).

He is referred to as the Second Coming of Jesus because he comes to a downtrodden people to lift them up to Godliness and Righteousness. He opens the eyes of the Blind, Deaf, and Dumb Negroes to Truth, and he raises the Spiritual and Mentally dead to life like Lazarus. If this man is not God, then we can certainly agree that he is a man of God. He was born February 26, 1877 in Mecca, Arabia. He was born for a special purpose in life, that of Resurrecting the world back to Righteousness and exposing Satan . His job is to make all truths plain so that the world can see the cause of all their problems. He must Resurrect a dead humanity back to spiritual life.

Some people wonder is he still physically alive, but Righteous people are never referred to as being dead because what they taught the public will live forever in the hearts and minds of the people, and life begins and end in the Heart of Man's Mind. So He Lives Forever! The name Fard means "Early Morning" thus we have one coming in the early morning of the seventh thousand year to bring about a complete change in the Thinking of the earth's population. His purpose is to re-establish the Kingdom of God on earth, as it was before the Making of the Devil. All those who refuse to accept righteousness during this transition of world powers will be destroyed.

He is called a master because there is no one capable of competing with him in wisdom. He is the wisest of this time and to come. His revelations about God and the Devil, the prophets and their histories, how the blackman was made a slave and kept in slavery today is unsurpassed. He spent 42 years in preparation for his mission. He traveled in and out of the United States for many years. He waited until after the Stock Market Crash of 1929 to announce who he was. The Bible states that he will come as a thief in the night (unaware).

On July 4, 1930 in Detroit, Michigan (at a meeting) he announced that he was the Supreme Being, the Supreme Being is God in person. The same God that created the universe, also creates human vessels to make his desires known. In the past it has been Abraham, Noah, Jesus, Muhammad, and now this man Fard Muhammad. It is important that you view him in the right lineage or you will miss his revelations of : Who the Devil Is, Heaven and Hell, Life after Death and many more revelations that will awaken a dead humanity. He stated that a change in world economic power is taking place and one need only watch and see.

Since that revelation the Japanese have taken over the lead in the industrial world, and the United States (Americans) are still fading in currency evaluation, production in quality goods and service, and morality in the work-place.

A final clarification on Fard Muhammad and his declaration of being God. All human beings are Gods and what makes it so is the Divine Creative Spirit of Almighty God that was deposited in us from birth. However, Man has been asleep to his Divinity for six-thousand years because the Devil has poisoned peoples minds against the truth in the Churches, Synagogue and Temples. The time has arrived for the public to wake up to who they really are, and this is the job of Master Fard Muhammad.

His first mission is to Wake Up The Blackman of America who has been not only asleep but dead for 400 years as to Who He Is, and anybody else on earth. But if you will notice, there is a gradual awakening of this slave. Once he is fully awake then the rest of the world will have no problem believing that God has appeared in the person of Master Fard Muhammad to put the Blackman back of top of Civilization, where he rightfully belong, and put the Devil where he belong.

Master Fard Muhammad is a friend to the Blackman and Woman of America and is not interested that you worship him as God, only start seeing the God in Yourself so that you can fulfill your destiny as God's Chosen People.

THE HON. ELIJAH MUHAMMAD AND
THE NATION OF ISLAM!

God in the person of Master Fard Muhammad converted approximately 25,000 black people to Islam during his three and half years in Detroit, but his primary convert and pupil was Elijah Poole, later to be known all over the world as Hon. Elijah Muhammad, the Messenger of Allah. Holy Quran 35:24 Surely we have sent thee with the truth as a bearer of good news and a Warner. And there is not a people but a Warner has not gone among them. Bible Malachi 4: 5-6 Behold, Before that great and dreadful day, I will send you Elijah the Prophet, and he shall turn the hearts of the fathers to the children and the hearts of the children to the father, lest I come and smite the earth with a curse.

The Whiteman has poisoned the minds of the people to the idea of accepting prophets. They feel that was during the old biblical days. He blinds them so that they can be destroyed with him in their filth. After Elijah Muhammad, there will be no need for another prophet because everything will be revealed. Elijah Muhammad was born Elijah Poole, October 7, 1897, in Sandersville, Ga. USA, A So Called Negro that have been lost in this cave called America for 375 years from his own native people. America is known spiritually as a cave because just as a cave shut out the light from its inhabitants; America has shut off the Negroes culturally, economically, religiously, educationally and every other way possible from the outside civilized life.

Elijah kept coming to the Temple of Islam until Fard Muhammad revealed to him that he was the Elijah in Malachi of the Bible and the Prophet Muhammad of the Holy Quran. The So Called Negroes were scriptural described as Arabs, and that our people had been hidden in scripture to protect our identity as God's People. All of this secrecy was done in order to allow the Devil to live out his time because once the Blackman wakes up to the Devil and his mischief, he will be ran off the planet. God comes to set up a new nation that will rule and live forever. He told Elijah that he was the one chosen to preach Islam to our people.

Islam means entire submission to the will of God. Islam is Peace. The one that submits to Islam bears witness that Allah is God and Muhammad is his last and greatest Apostle. Some of the prophets of Islam are Abraham, Moses, Jesus, Solomon, and Muhammad. Scriptural, Moses received the Torah, Jesus the Gospel, and, Muhammad received the Holy Quran. Elijah Muhammad received the last revelation of this world which was the Identity of God and the Devil. The statement from the Holy Quran 35:24 And there is not a people but a Warner has gone among them shows conclusively that Elijah Muhammad is a Divine Messenger because no one has ever come among the Negroes with a Divine Message.

Just as Allah used the Angel Gabriel to tell Prophet Muhammad that he was his Messenger and his mission was to raise a nation of Muslims. So it is that Fard Muhammad

Elijah Muhammad

(God In Person) told the Hon.Elijah Muhammad that he was his messenger and that his mission was to raise a nation of Muslims out of the so-called Negroes. Hon. Elijah Muhammad's mission was similar to Mohammed, only he comes at the end of the Devil's time to rule over the earth. Rev. 13: 18 Here is Wisdom. Let him that hath understanding count the number of the beast; for it is the number of a Man; and his number is six hundred, three score and six. It took six hundred years to make the Devil on the Isle of Patmos in the Aegean Sea , and three score is sixty times one hundred years , which equals six thousand years of rulership, and six equals the six days of the week, which spiritually means that he (devil) would rule for six days and the seventh day he would rest. In fact, the six day week and rest on sunday or the seventh day was patterned after his time of rule. One day with God is as a thousand years. The seventh day of rest is when the Blackman regains his power over the earth.

Now that the identity of the Hon. Elijah Muhammad is established as the Messenger of Allah, let us look at his mission. He was taught by Master Fard Muhammad for three and half years of Divine Wisdom. His guide is the Holy Quran and God. His purpose is to establish a Muslim Nation out of the So- Called Negroes, just as Moses established a nation out of the savage - minded whiteman, and Muhammad established a nation from the dis-functional, Nomadic Arabs. The concepts and Beliefs in Islam will remain the same. However, he must establish new dietary laws (No eating the Hog), He must restore the Negroes identity.

Institute new dress codes because the devil has the people naked and unfit to worship God. He has showed the world the shame of the Blackman and woman. A new Muslim nation must be established immediately!

When the Supreme Being came to America, he said that the So Called Negroes live in a cage that is 3,615,211 square miles, which is the circumference of the United states, and the Negro is walking backwards and forward in this cage like a lion. He has been doing this for four hundred years looking for the "Door" , the door is the door to his salvation which has finally come, and that door is Islam. If he would only walk in and through the door, he would find salvation to his soul.

The Nation of Islam was set-up by Master Fard Muhammad but Elijah Muhammad made it a nation for the Blackman of America with 63 years of hard work. The government, Nation of Islam is designed to give the Negroes their Original Names, Culture, History, and Flag. Also, teach them the Knowledge of Self, and the value of Freedom, Justice and Equality with other nations. But first, they must realize that they (Negroes) have been poisoned by the Devil in Mind and in Spirit. This re-orientation process is known as the Resurrection of The Dead 1 Cor 15 Ch. ! They must be cleaned up and made fit to rule themselves and then to rule others in Righteousness. Allah said that the Negroes minds were like a "Frozen Embryo" that must be thawed out and re-cycled into a New Way of Thinking.

Elijah Muhammad

The Devil in slavery said it this way "We have created an orbiting cycle that turns on its own axis forever, unless a phenomenon occurs and re-shifts the positions of the male and female savages". That phenomenon has occurred in the person Master Fard Muhammad and Elijah Muhammad.

✸ EUROPEANS ARE PEACE-BREAKERS ALL OVER THE WORLD!

Negro means Dead. The So Called Negroes are dead mentally and spiritually because they have buried their talents in the soil of America. The parable of the talents is a sign of the Negroes. Matthew 25:14 For the Kingdom of Heaven is like a man traveling into a far country, who called his servants, and delivered unto them his goods. One servant he gave five talents, another two, another one; each servant doubled his talents except the servant with one, he buried his talent in the ground. On returning the master blessed the other two servants and banished the third servant into outer darkness for not using the talent that God gave him.

Negroes in America are dead to the idea of building something for themselves. Like the Children of Israel, the Negroes have built up the cities of Pharaoh and have nothing for themselves as a reward of effort. Negroes get their identity from the Whiteman therefore it is easy to build for the Whiteman. Once they acquire a new Identity, then they will be able to build for self.

The problem is one of Identity and not a lack of Talents. The image of a Muslim must replace the identity or image of a slave. Let me tell you how the European gained control of the whole earth. Revelation 20:5 But the rest of the dead lived not again until the thousand years were finished. 1000 AD the European nation s were let loose out of their prison (Europe) to go forth and deceive the nations which are in the four quarters of the earth, spiritually known as Gog and Magog. Holy Quran titled " The Cave Chapter 18, section 11, footnote 1525," the ancestors of Gog and Magog are the Slav and Teutonic Races, and in the world domination , it is clearly   hinted   that the European Nation would dominate the whole world.

The methods that they would use is Tricks, Lies, and violent weapons. Tricknology is a science of tricks or deception and lies to fool people. When the traders landed in Africa among the Black people, they used Christianity to shield their intentions of making slaves out of black people by pretending that all men are from God and are brothers. They should love one another and that there was gold just lying on the ground in America. They should go there and get a sack and come back home; they never returned home.

The Europeans tricked the Indians with offerings of beads, gifts, whiskey and brotherhood saying they should all live together, as more and more settlers came, the Indians were pushed farther and farther from their land until the Whiteman with his rifles and cannons had conquered the Indians.

Peace-breakers

The Indians never knew what hit them. Now, they are all on reservations as a mockery ; Conquered by the Devil's tricks and lies or Tricknology. The Devil fights among his own people and in 1914 started World War One, which was a war of all the European nations fighting to divide up the spoil of the known conquered world. and in 1939 they started World War II which was a greater war in violence because they had developed the Atomic Bomb. The United States (Devils) dropped this bomb on innocent Japanese people with the excuse that this act brought the War to an early end.

Here is an article that described this deadly cowardly act.

"HE SAID IT"

PEARL HARBOR WAS NOT
AS CRUEL AS THE ATOMIC
BOMBING, THE ATOM BOMB
WIPED OUT EVERYTHING:
PEOPLE IN CHURCH, CHILDREN
IN KINDERGARTEN, EVEN
THEIR DOGS AND CATS. PEARL
HARBOR WAS TERRIBLE, BUT
NOT AS BAD AS THAT.

MAYOR HITOSHI MOTOSHIMA of Nagasaki, Japan, in an interview Wednesday. The United States dropped an Atomic Bomb on that city August 9, 1945, killing an estimated 140,000 people. The Japanese attack on Pearl Harbor , Hawaii, on Dec. 7, 1944 killed 2,400 people.

In 1949 they were at War with the Korean people, and then ten years later they were at war with the people of Vietnam. Their primary trick in these oriental countries is Divide and Conquer (Split the nation) into a South and North. Tell the did-satisfied leaders within the nation that you will support them against the other side, supply them money, weapons and material to fight against their brothers. What you have is North and South Vietnam, North and Peace-breakers

South Korea and the European(Devil) sitting and waiting and whoever wins he will be the arbitrator. Remember, he tell the dis-satisfied leaders that they should have a democratic government wherein they can have some voice. After the war, he is able to rule them both. The opposition party is backed politically by the European Government and is supplied weapons and propaganda material but if the Ruling party wins, then the European still wins because he can help him re-build his country. Divide and you will Conquer regardless of who win the war!

The mediator is perceived as a peacemaker and both sides agree to let the mediator or arbitrator settle the dispute with some type of agreement. Thus the peacemaker (European) is the cause of the trouble, but he has been able to divide the two nations, as well as settle their dispute. In the Middle East, Religion is the most explosive issue, so they (European) back up financially some Jews to overthrow the government of Palestine in Asia Minor, which was in the control of the Europeans after W.W.II, and was controlled by Great Britain.

Peace-breakers

The Europeans relinquished the government of Palestine to the Jews and legitimized it in the United Nation as a New sovereign nation "The Nation of Israel". They said that now this was the long-awaited homeland of the Jews of Scripture. This was also done in Kuwait and Iraq. Kuwait was a part of Iraq and after the Europeans had conquered the area they created an ANNEX to Iraq and called it Kuwait in 1961. Another example of Divide and Conquer among nations. This will continue to be until the world recognize the revelation that God has given through his servant Master Fard Muhammad. That revelation is that the Whiteman is the devil and he has Divided the world so that he can Conquer it.

The world population has been dead (unaware) to the knowledge of what were the intentions of the Europeans. However, they would live again, (Become mentally Aware) after the thousand year domination is up. After 1914, this period is known as the First Resurrection of The Dead, wherein God would makes all things plain and explain the tings that have not been known to Man.

REALITY OF GOD AND THE DEVIL

MATTHEW 24: 42-44 Watch, therefore; for ye know not what hour your Lord doth come. 43 But know this, that if the /householder/ had known in what watch the thief would come, he would have watched, and would not have /allowed/ his house to be broken in to. 44 Therefore be ye also ready ; for as in such an hour as ye think not, the

Son of Man cometh. It was in the darkest hour of the depression for the United States that the Son Of Man, Second Jesus, came in the person of Master Fard Muhammad and made himself known as the one prophesied in the Bible and Holy Quran that would come in the Last Days of Satan's World.

What is it besides scripture that indicates that this man is the return of Jesus? First, he comes at the end of Satan's rule to set-up a new pattern of living for the downtrodden. This new lifestyle will remove sickness and disease. He reveals the history of the Blackman and Woman of how they were made slaves, kept in slavery mentally and spiritually through tricks and false friendship. He explains how the Names, Culture, and Religion was taken from them by the Devil and replaced with his own Culture, Religion and Names. He explained how for the past 6,000 years the Devil has ruled in Unrighteousness, and now the Blackman must return to practicing Righteousness for his salvation . Islam was given to the Blackman for his religion, the principles are the same but the philosophy is different to meet the needs of the So-Called Negroes.

This is a New Islam and not the old orthodox Islam given to the Arabs of 1400 years ago. A new Islam will enable the Blackman to see God within himself just as a person can see the Devil within an individual that is practicing unrighteousness. Color has nothing to do with God , it is nature, and the practicing of righteous behavior.

Reality of God

There are three stages of spiritual development in Man; the first stage is the Animal level or the self-accusing spirit, the second is the human level, and the third is the Divine level. The Resurrection is designed to bring Mankind from the Animal level to the Divine Level. The so-called Negroes has rejected Master Fard Muhammad teachings because thy could not recognize him for who he really is (God In Person , like Jesus of 2,000 years ago). This is due to how they have been "Made in the Image Of the Whiteman", and as a result of what has been done to them is slavery. For what the American Whites have done to the Blackman, Allah has charged them with being the most wicked people on earth and the first to be destroyed as a people . The German Whites are second!

The Negroes have been abused and mistreated beyond recognition as the people of God. Scripture teaches that they would be among strangers for 400 years and the strangers that were responsible for this mistreatment are the Europeans collectively, and the American Whites particularly. It is because of this abuse, time in history, and their origin that Master Fard Muhammad has declared that these are the people of scripture that were Lost and now have been Found . Thus he declared, Revelation 21:3 And I heard a great voice out of heaven saying , Behold, the Tabernacle of God is with men, and he will dwell with them, and they shall be his people, and God himself shall be with them, and be their God. God Makes All Things New Revelation 21:5 !

They can't be judged as God's people now because they are not themselves. That is why the Coming of God is known spiritually as the Resurrection of The Dead. The dead must be raised before the world (White World) can be judged according to their deeds. Let us look at the Rich Man and Lazarus in scripture and see how it applies to the American Whiteman and the Blackman or Negro. Luke 16:19-31 There was a certain Rich Man, who was clothed in purple and fine linen, and fared sumptuously every day.

And there was a certain beggar, named Lazarus, who ate the droppings from the rich man's table, this beggar had sores from his head to his toes from mistreatment, the beggar died and was carried by the angels to the bosom of Abraham for peace and comfort. The Rich Man also died and was buried in hell; in hell he lifted up his eyes, being in torment and seeth Abraham afar off, and Lazarus in his bosom. He cried out to let Lazarus bring his some water or go to his brothers and tell them how terrible this place was. Abraham refused by saying that if his brothers did not listen to all of their prophets, then sending Lazarus would do no good.

The meaning of the parable is as follows; The so-called Negroes (Lazarus) have suffered as a beggar in America, and as a result of this mistreatment and suffering has died as a Self Sufficient People. The Rich Whiteman of America has eaten sumptuously every day in every conceivable way and mistreated this poor beggar. The Rich Man died also, and lost his wealth and world power due to the way he mis-used people all over the world.

Lazarus

The Rich Man in hell , saw Lazarus in the bosom of Abraham (Protection of God) and cried out for help from his brethren (Europeans). However God said that they (European have had Moses and the Prophets for Four-Thousand Years) and if they did not hear them, they will not do right if one rose from the dead, like Lazarus.

The other parable of Lazarus is John 11:11-44 When Jesus came to Lazarus, he said that our friend Lazarus sleepeth. He had lain in his grave for four days already, and Jesus said loose him, and let him go. The sleep is mental sleep and the grave is the Mind, and the four days is four hundred years being dead in America. The Blackman has a through knowledge of Hell, so let us study the true meaning of Heaven on earth.

CHAPTER IX.

HEAVEN IS A STATE OF MIND!

Heaven and Hell begin and end in this life. They are States of Mind. They are the re-action of conditions that affect our lives. They are the substance that a Righteous or Evil person receive in this world. Heaven is the peace that comes from a person's soul that is at rest with God and his laws. When one's soul is at rest with God, this is the highest spiritual bliss that one can attain in this life on earth. There is no grief, fatigue, or toil, and the heart is purified of all rancor and jealousy. Peace and security reigns all around you, this is Heaven! Heaven, heaven is not a place, it is essentially a state of mind. It is everlasting as long as you are in God, and obeying his laws.

Hell is also a State of Mind. Hell was not meant for punishment or torture, but rather for purification, in order to make a person fit for spiritual advancement. The idea underlying hell is that whoever has wasted his opportunity to do good shall under the inevitable law which makes every Heaven and Hell
man taste of what he has done "be given another chance by undergoing a course of treatment, sometimes called a chastisement for their spiritual diseases." Individuals with a Reprobate Mind practicing such diseases as Cheating, Lying, Murdering, Envy, and Jealousy must be purified or destroyed, hell is for their own benefit and not their detriment.

Heaven and Hell

Heaven is having power to accomplish what you will in a right and beneficial manner. God has come to give the Blackman that power. The power is Spiritual Power that comes from practicing the Word of God. It is power that manifest as Mind Power. Mental or Mind Power is the greatest power on earth. From Mind Power comes the ability to analyze correctly and understand problems. From Spiritual Power comes the development of inner faculties like Mental Telepathy, Precognition, Conception, Visualization and complete self-knowledge.

Heaven is having the ability and resources to do something with yourself, if you are not lazy. The parable of the talents in Matthew 25: 14-129 explains it well. The Kingdom of Heaven is like a man traveling into a far country, who called his servants and delivered unto them his goods. One servant he gave five talents and he doubled it; another two talents and he doubled it; another he gave one talent and he buried it because he felt that it was not enough to do anything with. The Lord blessed the other servants with more wealth, and condemned the one servant for not trying to profit with what little talent that he had. So it is with the So Called Negroes of America, they have buried their talents in the soil of America, and they will not even Try To Build A House For Themselves With What Little Talent That They Possess.

The Blackman does not realize that as long as they continue to Bury their resources i.e. Money, Brain Power, and Skills, they will always remain powerless as a people, and in Hell.

If the Blacks of America separated themselves long enough to build up a power base of money, then it would be easy to get true friends with other nations. But, Power is not a gift, it must be earned. Power is acquired by separation and mutual cooperation between nations of equals. No powerful nation ever shared its wealth with its slave. The Blackman must become an equal through hard work with its own talents, and not by burying its talents in another nation. Blackman Use Your Talents To Build Your Own Nation!

In order to build a nation for Black People, there will have to be some independent leaders that are not afraid to speak on behalf of Blacks. Most black leaders are stool pigeons, and spies for the Whiteman. The Same as In Physical Slavery!! The Leader must be able to establish Law among the people or a governmental framework to work from i.e. Islam. No nation can be a nation without some Land. This land is what gives sovereign rights of legitimacy. This is only a sketch that could be done immediately with some economics that is already in the whiteman's banks. If the Blackman does not act today, it may be too late tomorrow. Remember the 1929 Stock Market Crash, it could happen again.

The Laws that would govern the nation are the Laws of God, which means a Religious nation, a righteous nation. Anything that is against scripture is forbidden in this government. That means there would be no more murder, stealing, cheating, adultery, insanity, drunkenness, or rape.

121

Heaven and Hell

This is Heaven, and it can be done overnight if the people wanted a government of this kind.

The story or picture that the so-called Negroes are to follow is Moses and the Children of Israel, which is really a parable of the Blackman in America. The Jews were never in bondage for 400 years to anyone, that were the Negroes in America. The White Jews were never Born in a society where they did not know their roots, or culture, or heritage, they have always known who they were; That happened to the Negroes of America, who lost their identity!

The Jews interpreted scripture in their favor to show that they were the Chosen People of God, and were abused and persecuted for their Faith. NOT TRUE! That happened to the Blackman of America who was denied having a Religion, for over three hundred years, couldn't read scripture or was killed, and eventually was allowed into the Whiteman's Religion so that he could worship him as God, and not the real God, Allah! The BlACKMAN STILL IS NOT IN HIS OWN RELIGION, Let Us Get The Story Straight.

The Blackman is in Hell, and not Heaven. He could be in heaven if he would wake up and start producing a nation of his own, but he must have the right State of Mind. God is her to give him that right State of Mind i.e. Islam.

COLONIALISM IS A WAY OF LIFE FOR EUROPEANS!

When the whiteman evolved out of the Dark Ages (Cave Days) the Age of Enlightenment (Renaissance), the Blackman (Muslims) had already built beautiful cities in Cordoba, Spain, and Morocco. The Muslims were building in Europe. Moses and Jesus were Muslims. A Muslim means one that submit to Almighty God to do his Will. Religions are established by a Man, given a name, and then confusion sets in , if one does not call God by the Name that the founder of the Religion said that it was. White People took the religion that Paul gave them (Not Jesus), and used it as a tool to enslave the minds of people that they came in contact with in Europe, Africa and Asia.

Emperor Aurelius Constantine (AD 306-337) accepted Christianity and made it the State or National Religion of the Roman Empire, with the seat in Rome and it is still in effect today. Why is not the Capitol of Christianity in Jerusalem ? I will tell you why---because Jesus was not a Gentile or Caucasian representing their Religion. They rejected Jesus and now are using what he said to make people think that they are his people. Jesus was a Jewish Blackman who lived in and around Jerusalem all of his life, his body is supposed to be embalmed and in a tomb to last for 10,000 years , the Jews claim him to indicate that he is one of them. But these Jews (White People) in Jerusalem today are not the real Jews. They not only have claimed Jesus but all of the Prophets and the Holy Land. This will be the Last War!!

Colonialism

White People have colonized the Holy Land for their own personal use and heritage, they have taken over South Africa, South America, North America, including Asia and the Pacific. They have truly fulfilled scripture wherein in Genesis 1:26 Let them have dominion over the fish, and over the fowl of the air, and over the cattle, and over all the earth, and over every creeping thing that crept upon the earth. This is one method that they used in conquering other people. The Roman Empire is their greatest empire for power and everything European springs from that foundation.

If the Romans captured an African Nation, it was either destroyed or remained a colony of Rome. The Roman made them speak their language, changed their names to Roman names, killed most of the men and impregnated the women with Roman offspring. Removed their culture completely and dug up all of the producing soil on the land and poured cement so nothing could ever grow on that soil again. Once thoroughly indoctrinated into the Roman Culture then they were made second-class citizen or slaves to serve the Roman Empire. They could never become actual Roman citizen because the nation was Caucasian! This is something that the Negro just can't seem to understand. Why he can't be a full-fledged American Citizen. Colonialism is not God's Way but the European Way.

God did not intend for them to kill and take other peoples home from them. He wanted to experiment in Man living under different cultures and natures of Man, although he knew the outcome before it took place, but the primary way the average person learns is through Experience, and A Wise Person learns through Observation and Education. It is sad when one has to experience something before one can learn from it .

Their is a Revolution going on in the world and it is A Mental Revolution. The entire planet is undergoing a CHANGE because of this Divine Knowledge about God and the Devil. God come to set the record of Who Is The First Man, Heaven and Hell, Who is the Troublemaker. What is the right Religion? Christianity is not the right religion for the Blackman because it enslaves his mind to lies. It is a slave-making religion because Whites are God's People and Blacks are slaves. The purpose of allowing white people to rule this earth was only an experiment. To learn how to live under Unrighteousness. He has done a good job. These revelations from God is setting free the minds of people that have been captured psychologically for thousands of years.

Heaven is having the Knowledge of God, Self, and Others. The absence or ignorance to that knowledge signifies Hell for that person or nation. The Negroes are in hell because they lack this vital knowledge of Self. However, the Hon.Elijah Muhammad has laid the foundation for a new nation, and if as Moses, he is not able to see the new nation, it must be maintained the same way that he laid the foundation which is: The spiritual base Islam must be taught the same way, he taught it. Second, the believers must be taught and trained the knowledge of our

Colonialism

Culture. Third, Establish some businesses and economics of
our own. These three principles are A Must To Maintain
after the Messenger if the Nation of Islam is to survive. The
Blackman of America is building a nation, and not just
establishing Islam in the West. Some people feel that is what
is taking place in America, the establishment of another
Religion. Islam has been in this country for years, but the
Blackman brought it to the forefront because he needed a
total concept of life to articulate his views.

The foundation for the Negroes to build on is;
Change Your Name from the whiteman's name to one of
God's names or attributes. Names represents ownership and
as long as black people are using white peoples names , it
indicates that they are still the property of white people.
(Spiritually if not Physically). Next, Get out of Christianity
and into your own religion Islam. Change your Dietary
Laws and stop eating the Swine (Hog). Love and Respect
your Brothers and Sisters. Build Your Own Economy to
protect yourself against the day of want, that is coming
upon America.

Heaven is having your own nation to support you
and your kind. Hell is living in another Man's house (nation)
and dependent on what he gives you economically,
politically, morally, and culturally. THE BLACKMAN
MUST WAKE UP MENTALLY---time is running out!

THE LAST MESSAGE

John 8:32 Ye Shall Know The Truth and the Truth Shall Set You Free. Negro Is an Invention Of The Whiteman. There are three stages to raising the blackman back to spiritual life, these stages are known as The Resurrection Of The Dead. The first stage is the laying of the foundation or the Nation of Islam. The second stage is the establishment of the Belief and actions of a Muslim. The third stage is to reward each believer according to their works, and not according to their beliefs, desires, looks or ambition. The nation must be established on a solid foundation of Truth. If the Negroes refuse to build a nation for themselves and continue to rely on the USA government for their sustenance, then their death is permanent.

In the Last Days, each nation will be rewarded according to their deeds, and if the Blackman has no nation, and is practicing the same habits and ways of the Whiteman, then he will be given the same reward. The Last Message to come to the Blackman is ISLAM, take it or leave it! The Holy Quran states the Last Message in this manner: The Doom 45:28-29 And Thou shall see every nation kneeling down. Every nation will be called to its record. This day you are requited for what you did. This is our record that speaks against you with Truth. Surely we wrote what you did. The record or book of each individual or nation is called into account for is his actions. On the Day of Resurrection, the effects of a person's deeds will be revealed to its fullest.

The Last Message

A person's evil deeds are like unto a prison, because it hampers his progress and keeps his faculties shut up from doing great and good deeds. Whereas the person whose book or record is of good deeds will find himself in the highest places because by good deeds the faculties given to Man find their highest development. That each nation has a book bears out the truth that the impression of what a people do is left on their national life, and nations like people are judged for what they do; Lo, Read My Book 69-19 the evil doer is made to say "O would that my book had never been given me, and I had not known what my account was! The evil that was done to the Blackman and Woman (Making them Negroes) can never be repaid!

The main reason that God came to the Negroes is to restore their Identity. If their true identity is not accepted and acted upon; then it would be useless to build a nation on the mental foundation that the whiteman has created (Negro Foundation), because they still would not know who they really are. The Knowledge of Self or the Knowledge of Your True Identity is the first step in being a civilized nation or person. A nation cannot be built without its own Identity. That is why the teachings of Islam are so important to the so-called Negroes because it gives him his identity. No other science, religion, or history is complete unless a person is able to visualize himself in that science, religion, or history in a true sense. The Blackman has been given a false sense of identity.

The words of Islam have been accepted mentally by the Blackman, but they have not penetrated to the heart. In order to build a nation for self, the words must be accepted mentally and spiritually until the words penetrate your heart and give you a new identity; based on actions. God must give us a Muslim Mentality or Muslim Mind , then and only then will the Negroes be qualified to build a Muslim Nation in America. Allah does not intend for the Blackman to be eating swine, drinking wine, cursing, and swearing at his wife, fornicating, committing adultery, lying, and cheating, in this nation. This is A Righteous Nation! Every man and woman will be rewarded according to his Works. Belief counts for nothing unless carried into practice.

In this book, spiritually, Negro means Dead! This is based upon the past present, and future deeds of the Negroes in America. After 400 years of labor the Negroes are still trying to survive and the Whiteman is Rich. Ezekiel's vision 37:1-10 of the Dry Bones in the Valley depicts how dead the Negroes have become as a nation. The Son of Man (Master Fard Muhammad), starts to blowing the wind (Teachings of Islam) upon the slain Minds of the Negroes so that they might live. The Trumpet that is sounding is the deaf ears of the Negroes is Islam as Taught by the Hon. Elijah Muhammad (Not Orthodox Islam). The Grave that they are lying in is Christianity. They must be raised from the false concepts (God, Jesus, and Prophets are all White) and get into their own Religion.

The Last Message

The restoration of the House of Israel for the Children of Israel means that the Hon. Elijah Muhammad must restore a new house "Nation of Islam that will restore the Negro's National Heritage, Identity. Religion, Culture, Names, and a correct interpretation of scripture. The dry bones in the valley represents a dead nation within another nation that must be resurrected by God and his Messenger. The people have been slain and scattered all over the valley until they had no flesh and had become bones. God restored them back as a nation by teaching them the Truth. The Children of Israel had been taught by their enemies Lies that put them in a condition of being spiritually dead. This new teachings will resurrect their minds if they believe it just as they believed the lies of the Devil.

The Hon. Elijah Muhammad has restored the dry bones back together as a nation (Nation Of Islam) to live forever. Allah (Master Fard Muhammad) should be praised forever for coming and giving life, and resurrecting the dead from their graves of ignorance. NEGRO MEANS A DEAD STATE OF MIND!

CHAPTER X

SLAVERY LAWS AND CHRISTIANITY KEEPS THE BLACKMAN A MODERN-DAY SLAVE!

One of the problems with the Blackman and Woman of America is that they lack a true knowledge of God and his religion. The knowledge of God is the greatest and most vital of all knowledge to possess. A True knowledge of God is the basis of all belief systems in every religion in the world. Ninety-eight percent of the people of the earth are without this knowledge of God. A lack of this knowledge is what enables the Devil to boast in scripture that he will attract two-thirds of the stars with his TALE (not tail) because the real devil does not have a tail.

Christianity uses Jesus Christ, a righteous man to shield their dirt, lies, and falsehood by twisting up his teachings. They re-arrange his teachings to enslave the minds of people of color all over the world. Christianity is the whiteman (Devil) religion. They have murdered black people in the name of Christianity and Jesus, burned and castrated blacks to preserve their purity of Faith. They (whites) do not want you worshipping with them on Sunday but yet you (blacks) think that you are all equal in God's eyesight. NOT TRUE! God does not equalize the Whiteman with his Children. He has condemned them to burn in a Lake of Fire "Read Your Bible".

131

Slaves by Law

You are still enslaved by they, and mesmerized by their wealth and different looks, but God has a place for you and a place for them YOU ARE NOT EQUAL IN RELIGION OR NOTHING ELSE! There are some societies that worship the Sun, Moon, Snakes, Cows, and fire as signs of God or the real God. In this society, many worship Jesus as God, this is a real problem! I have mentioned it before and I will mention it again , the Bible tells us how to recognize God . 1Cor. 3:16 Know Ye Not that Ye Are the Temple Of God, and that the Spirit of God dwells in You?

That is a question, If the Blackman or so-called Negroes knew that "He Was God, and Not The Whiteman" then all of his problems would be over. Because he would realize that to serve the whiteman is to serve a graven image, and to disgrace himself. He would realize that Almighty God could not Bless him in the position of A Slave, because it would be blessing the whiteman, since he still is the whiteman' slave.

The Negro does not know who he is , and as a result of this self-ignorance, he is in effect worshipping the Devil instead of worshipping God. To know God, he must know himself; to know himself is to serve and build for self. Doing for Self is a form of self-worship in a true spiritual sense. The creator deposited this creative spirit within the mind of the Blackman to be used for himself and kind. The Negroes are not worshipping God because they do not care anything about themselves; they care more about the devil and his desires than their own.

JESUS WAS NOT A WHITEMAN, The reason the Blackman primary problem is Religion is because he lost his identity in religion, he lost his spiritual connection with God in religion, he became blind, deaf, and dumb, in the Christian Religion. He started believing that God was in the sky and the devil was in the ground. in religion. He Must Wake Up Spiritually to the Truth. There is more confusion about Jesus coming back to life and saving people than the national debt.

The past history of Jesus of two-thousand years ago was a Sign of Something To Come in The Future. Jesus was born out of Wedlock and this was a sign of a future people of Jesus being born out of Wedlock (So Called Negroes). Jesus tried to resurrect the Black Jews to a higher understanding about God. Master Fard Muhammad (Second Jesus) is resurrecting the Blackman of America to a higher understanding about God and Self. Jesus was unable to convert the Jews to whom he was sent. On the other hand, the Second Jesus, Master Fard Muhammad will convert the whole world because he will open the eyes of people to things that had been hidden for six-thousand years.

Some notables people that have done great works since being raised from the dead in the Nation of Islam are: Hon. Elijah Muhammad, Minister Louis Farrakhan, Malcolm X Shabazz, and Muhammad Ali. These are just a few of the Black leaders that were mentally and spiritually dead before the teachings of Islam resurrected their minds.

They were so-called Negroes and is a testimony to this great and powerful truth that our Savior Master Fard Muhammad brought to the Blackman of America. This truth and the practicing of this truth is all that is necessary to uplift a fallen nation, CHRISTIANITY IS NOT THE WAY!

SLAVERY REFORM LAWS

One of the biggest tricks they the Whiteman has sprung on the Blackman is to make him think that he is now a "Citizen" of the United States. The whiteman has learned that to keep the Blackman enslaved after slavery was abolished was to do it Legally. Neither Abraham Lincoln nor his running mate Andrew Johnson was trying to free the slaves but rather unite the nation. After Lincoln was assassinated, then President Johnson took office and his statement about the Negroes was " Damn the Negroes, I wish to God every head of a family in the United States had one slave)black) to take the drudgery and menial work off the family He signed into law the Thirteenth Amendment abolishing slavery, in order to unite the nation on a new industrial economic base for the nation!!

In 1865, Congress passed a Civil Rights Act (Which President Johnson vetoed, saying it was unconstitutional) which besides declaring that Negroes were citizens of the United States, denied the states the power to restrict their right to testify in court and to hold property.

"One hundred years later President Lyndon B. Johnson was still signing Civil Rights Acts declaring what are the rights of Minorities or Blacks in this country. (History Repeats, unless You Change your Ways and Habits, but white people will not change their ways toward black people). The Law passed that would enable a black to hold property was a little too late for Dred Scott. In June 1866, Congress passed and submitted to the states, a new amendment to the Constitution, the Fourteenth Amendment.

This Amendment gave a broad definition of American Citizenship. All persons born or naturalized in the United States, and subject to the jurisdiction there of, are citizens of the United States, and of the states wherein they reside. No state shall make or enforce any law that deprive the privileges or immunities of any citizens, nor deprive any citizen of life, liberty of property. Now here is the trick!!

Dred Scott was a slave that tried to petition his freedom after his master died , but the Law read that you must be a citizen to even put in a petition against the state for your freedom or to own property. A Slave did not have access to a Court of Law because He was a slave. Now, the Devil says that you are a citizen if born in the United States and this was intended for the white immigrants coming from abroad to settle in this land, so that they could vote, and enjoy the privileges of being an American.

When this law was passed, black people still could not vote, they just passed Voting Rights Laws in 1963.

135

Slavery Laws

Segregation was in full force and the Jim Crow laws didn't come to an end until after the 1960's and the sit-ins and Bus-Ins by black protesters. Blacks were being lynched whenever the Whiteman felt the urge. The Whiteman had children by the Black woman whenever he pleased and still is to this day. The Blackman was not given his name back after this Citizenship law was passed. He was not re-taught his Religion, Culture, or given his rightful identity. If a person is incarcerated for 300 years and you let him out of prison (slavery), then you must return all of his goods back to him or you are considered a robber yourself. You must return his Goods, and the goods (Name, Culture, Religion, Flag, and Starter Money or Reparation) was not returned to the Blackman after stating that he was now a citizen.

THAT IS A TRICK, HE WAS NOT A CITIZEN THEN NOR IS HE ONE NOW! THE BLACKMAN IS A CITIZEN By-law, which means that if you have a brother-in -law, he is not your real brother, only through Marriage. Once the Marriage dissolves, he has no relationship to you at all. So it is with the Whiteman and his relationship to the Blackman. By- Law the two must get along and perform civil duties like civilized people or citizens, in order for the government to function. WITHOUT LAW THE GOVERNMENT COULD NOT FUNCTION AND EXIST. So the whiteman always uses the law constantly, changing and re-changing in order to keep the Blackman in his place (on the bottom) and himself on the Top. He does this by Using The Law.

Black people are not citizens by naturalized birth, but by the Laws of the Amended Constitution. White People according to them are the naturalized citizens.

1955 DESEGREGATION OF THE SCHOOLS

The time is approaching 400 years of being in a strange land with strangers (Genesis 15:13) and being afflicted . At this point in time , the slaves, are totally blind, deaf, and dumb tot the knowledge of himself and the outside world of his kind. The slave has been segregated every since he has been in America, and now the Whiteman most effective trick is called INTEGRATION. A trick is a deceptive strategy used to deceive a person or people. The worst nightmare of the Whiteman is that the Blackman be free and out from under his control here in America, because it would mean the end of his power to rule and the beginning of the Blackman's time to rule.

So, they came up with this strategy called Integration. The purpose is to keep the slave close and provide minimal support to keep them within the framework of their government. Integration would allow Whites to control every aspect of the slave's life. Integration is based on mental and spiritual , and not physical control. If the blacks were allowed to SEPARATE, then they could build their own society.

Let us review how Integration worked during the 1955 Desegregation of the Schools.

Slavery Laws

The 1954 Brown vs. Board of Education of Topeka Kansas was a case that challenged the Separate But Equal school system and the Supreme Court declared that there was no such thing as Separate But Equal and that it was unconstitutional. The schools must be" Integrated with all deliberate speed." The Blacks were happy and felt that they had won a major victory. But let us analyze the results of that decision; the curriculum is controlled by whites and it did not include any studies on black people beyond the cotton fields, but rather Negro History to re-inforce a negative stereotype. They instituted Busing which takes black children out of their own community into white areas. They destroyed the black community by spreading the people all over wherein they could not build an economic base for themselves.

Integration really means dis-integration for the Blackman. Education is a tool for molding and shaping the Mind. Roman history was taught to the Blackman as history. They shaped the education, religion and all areas of life for the Blackman to live in his integrated society. They started organizations like NAACP, URBAN LEAGUE, and the CHURCH to control the thoughts and movements of the Blackman. The strategy of Integration has fooled the Blackman and Woman into thinking that what the Whiteman has is also his too. NOT TRUE!

1964 CIVIL RIGHTS ACT PROHIBITS DISCRIMINATION!

In 1964, the news of the Blackman and Woman's mistreatment during the marches, sit-ins, dog bite, police brutality and other atrocities became known to black nations in Asia and Africa . America sought to improve its reputation and image by passing a new Civil Rights legislation. This Civil Rights Act outlawed Discrimination in all public accommodations, such as hotels, restaurants, theaters, and credit unions. If found practicing discrimination then federal funds could be withheld from "Federally Funded Programs." Keep in mind that the slave was suppose to be free from the days of Dred Scott.

What citizen has to have laws written for him/her over and over through the years? It is obvious that Black People are not citizens in America, but more or less Indentured Servants or Citizen By Law. Don't forget that White People abused everybody ; Ask the Arabs of Desert Storm, or the Japanese, or the Eskimos when they spill oil over their land and don't want to pay for damages to their environment. The air is poison from pollution, and the grass is poisoned from pesticides, and the water is poisoned from chemicals and there are still Negroes talking about this is a Great Society. It Is Time To Wake Up.

The Blackman has never been in such a terrible shape mentally and it has cause his Mind To Be Captured by these following conditions, and thus keeps him in perpetual slavery.

HABITS THAT DESTROY THE BLACK COMMUNITY.

1. Christianity
2. Drugs i.e. Cocaine, Heroin, Alcohol
3. No Economy
4. Poor self-esteem
5. Lack of Unity
6. No Culture
7. No History
8. No National Agenda
9. Low Morals
10. Fornication
11. Adultery
12. Violent Acts: Murder, Gambling, Lying, Stealing, Cheating , and Sexual deviation (Sodomy).
13. Eating Swine, Smoking cigarettes
14. Lack of A Strong self-image
15. Lack of a Good Dietary Law

These problems must be remedied before the Blackman can be set free to build a society that he can call his own.

CHAPTER XI.

CORRECT MEANING OF SCRIPTURE

In order to fully understand why the Blackman was kidnapped from his home in Africa and made a slave in the western hemisphere by white people, nations fighting against nations, and generally no peace on earth in the last six-thousand years then one must understand the true identity of the Whiteman in Scripture. The Bible states it this way in Chapter 20, verses t and 8, And when the thousand years are ended (From 2,000 AD to 1,000 AD), Satan shall be loosed out of his prison, and shall go out to deceive the nations which are in the four quarters of the earth, God and Magog, to gather them together to battle; the number of whom are as the sands of the earth.

The Holy Quran states it this way in Chapter 18 verse 94. They said: O Dhu-l-garnain, Gog and Magog do mischief in the land. May we then pay thee tribute on condition that thou raise a barrier between us and them? 1523 This verse brings us face to face with the all important subject , viz., the identity of Gog and Magog. We are told that Gog and Magog will again be let loose in the latter days. When Gog and Magog are let loose they will sally forth from every point of eminence, and they will dominate the world . " They will drink the water of the whole world", the ancestors of Gog and Magog are the Slav and Teutonic Races (White People), and in the world domination of Gogand Magog is thus clearly hinted the domination of

Correct Interpretation

the" European Nations over the whole world, and the prophecy has thus found fulfillment in our days. The Quran and Bible makes it clear that Gog and Magog or Satan is none other than the European Nations or White People.

The" letting loose on the world" was their leaving the confinement of Europe and causing nations to fight against nations. Now, the Devil was given six-thousand years to rule the earth, and then after that time, the Blackman would regain control of his home (earth) again. We are in that transition period in history wherein the earth is being reclaimed by its rightful owner. Holy Quran Chapter 2, Section 4, verse 30 titled Greatness of Man and Need of Revelation. And when thy Lord said to the Angels, I am going to place a ruler in the earth, they said: Wilt thou place in it such as make mischief in it and shed blood? And we celebrate Thy praise and extol Thy holiness. He said: Surely I know what you know not. God 's purpose with Man is to make him Perfect through Trials.

The Whiteman is a trial for the Blackman in Righteousness! Everything that God say "Thou Shall Not Do, the Whiteman say "Thou Will Do". In the Garden of Eden, Man is warned to stay away from the Tree of Good and Evil, but God has never restricted Good from Man but only Evil. Man is entitled to all the benefits of nature, but he has been warned repeatedly against the Tree of Sin, tree of Death, because Sin destroys the Soul. Sin is what brought Man down from Grace. The Devil goes around the planet sowing evil suggestions in the hearts and minds of Correct Interpretation

142

people (Pornography, Prostitution, Gambling and glamorizes it in the movies as being normal)God's revelations are what strengthen a Man's Faith and give him the strength to resist the Devil and his suggestions. It is by following the Divine Guidance sent by God through his prophets that Men will attain to Perfection. Man's state of perfection is ; There is no Fear, nor grief, and Man is at peace with himself.

In order for Man to truly know himself and to attain to perfection or greatness, God has established a two-way method of knowing something. First, God makes a creature, human , or plant to study in real life. Second, he implants within that item Divine Knowledge to relate with the physical world outside of self, called instincts. If a person cannot instinctively know what to do then the third method is Divine Guidance from God.

If a human being cannot find God within self, and cannot experience God through Divine Guidance then that person does not want God and must suffer the consequences of not believing.

WAR OF ARMAGEDDON

The War Of Armageddon is a mental and spiritual war wherein the people of earth must decide on whom they will serve---God or the Devil. Righteousness or Unrighteousness. From the beginning of this six thousand years dispensation of Adam ands Eve being dispelled from Correct Interpretation the Garden of Eden , evil has prevailed over good, now this is the final judgment. There is no more extension of time for people that reject God's message. The War of Armageddon is about restoring the righteous back to their rightful place of ruling the earth in peace. The earth has been ruled by a devil for thousand of years and it is easy to see. Look at the murdering of the people, lying, fornicating, and robbery occurring by the minute in societies all over the world. The devil is frantically trying to keep the people asleep and dead to the times by providing more Sports and Play, Entertainment on a 24 hour basis, and Sex to deaden the Mind to the seriousness of the hour.

This battle of keeping the people asleep as to the Hour or Doom of this world is known as the War of Armageddon. It is a Mental War and not a war of guns and bombs as in W.W.I, and W.W.II. This Mental war will be for the Minds of the People of Earth and this will be WW III, it has already started. It began in 1914, and the end is not predicted time-wise because it is the Seventh-Day or a thousand year transition. But, one can visualize the transition from the changes that are taking place in the world. The Mental Revolution is to change the hearts and minds of people to see that there is only "One Nation" on earth and that is the Human Nation. After the people wake up to the fact that the Mental Cause of all their problem is a flawed evil conceptual viewpoint of Satan, and change to God's conceptual viewpoint of life, then the Judgment will set in, and the power of Satan to rule over the Minds of people will be broken!

Satan cannot rule your Mind if you refuse to accept his Way of Life, his thoughts, his plans, his ideas of pleasure, and he cannot rule your mind most of all, if you accept God. The War Of Armageddon is All In The Mind. The battlefield of the War of Armageddon is your Mind, and when the Blackman was made blind, deaf, and dumb in slavery, he had no idea of the power of his Mind, nor of how to communicate with God. He was considered a "Spook" a person easily frightened or startled. He worshipped anything that fascinated his imagination. When it was lighting and thundering, no one could talk because God was talking. He would hide in the closet if there was a closet. If it was raining and the Sun shining at the same time the Devil was beating his wife.

So, when the Whiteman gave him a Bible (He couldn't read) and explained to him that he would die and go to heaven , he didn't know any better. When the Whiteman explained that Heaven was in the sky and Hell in the ground, he was ignorant to scripture, and still is today! The War of Armageddon is here to remove all spiritual mythology and deception that has been poisoning the minds of God People. Once spiritual truth is understood then the fundamental facts of the universe must be re-taught to the Blackman and Woman.

The Blackman and Woman is not a Race but a Nation. The First and only Nation. All of the Races evolves from the Black Nation (Indians, Japanese, Chinese, and Whites). A Race has a beginning and a end. The Blackman has no recorded beginning nor an end. The history of the

Correct Interpretation

Blackman is written every 25,000 years in advance (in accordance with the circumference of the earth). This is how Prophets, Forecasters, and Wise men are able to know the future because it is already written up in a book.

In order to get this book, which is known as Scripture, or a script of writing, the clergymen, scientist, or rulers at that time gather the forecasters together and tell them to collect the" Thoughts Of The People" for the next history. The people are unaware that it is their thoughts that makes the history. The dissatisfied and the satisfied thoughts of the people is what brings about a change in society. A society that is 30% dis-satisfied can change the whole society. Man Is God and he creates his own Heaven or Hell. Once gathered and compiled, the Thoughts become the history or future for the people as to what is going to happen. What the Whiteman is doing was known to the scripture-writers before he was made by the Blackman.

Again, people did not know and still do not know to this day that it is their own thoughts and deeds that determine their future. Most people think that it is God that is doing things in their lives, not realizing that they are the God doing it. The War of Armageddon is designed to stop this confusion within the Mind of Man, so he can accept himself for who he truly is, a Self-Creator that creates his own heaven. As history evolves, certain portions of the book is given out to the people by a Prophet. This is done so that the works of the past period of history can not be duplicated; these new people will have to do their work without the aid of a previous civilization's knowledge. That

146

is another reason why no human being comes back to life after one is dead physically because each generation must perform its own work and not another in its place. The War of Armageddon is to Wake Up the Sleeping Blackman that his time has come to build his own society , but first free your Mind!

LIFE AFTER DEATH

Death is a stage in evolution. Just as dust is evolved the man, so it is that from the deeds which he does, evolves the higher or lower man. Death is only a stage in growth or regression. As from the small life germ the man grows up, but he does not lose his individuality, although he undergoes many changes, so from this man is evolved the higher man. His attributes changes and he is made to grow into what he cannot conceive at the present. Each stage of growth is a form of death and growing out of that stage is a form of new life. A Life After Death is normally a world of new advancement and progress, and the old world becomes insignificant. Physical death settles all things and God did not ordain any physical dead people to come back among the living and give instructions to live people (including Jesus).

In fact, Jesus said Let The Dead Bury The Dead, meaning that his message was for the living and not dead people. Life After Death refers to giving life to a mental and spiritually dead people that have been lost for over 400 years from their own nation. Life after Death is Mental

Correct Interpretation

Progress after being dead to the knowledge of God and the Devil. It does not mean that after you die, you will go to another place in another sphere of life. This is the home for human beings and God is the spiritual home for the Righteous because God guides them while they are alive on earth. When one is physically dead, he is done!

The Hereafter should be understood because it does not mean that after you die, you will go to heaven or hell . It means that after the veil of falsehood have been removed from your mind, and you are raised up in the knowledge of God and his commandments, that is the Hereafter. After the Devil in your life comes God--that is the Hereafter. When Satan has been removed as the ruling power of your mind and God begins to rule your mind with truth--that is the Hereafter. Nothing takes place after one is physically dead.

The reason why man is so estranged from God is because of material greed. America and its Allies are so engrossed in the contest of manufacturing that they have no thought of God . A great world-wide conflict is going on for wealth and more wealth, and God is the only one that can restore the balance to the world. Material benefits have turned man into the enemy of man. The day of peace for this world will come about when man realizes that there is only one nation, and that is the human nation, and the first human nation was the black nation.

Satan is working against the plans of God (Resurrecting The Dead Black Nation To Life) but he will be brought to disgrace. Material acquisitions are used as an inducement to poor people to allure them away from God and his plan of salvation which is to give them Life After Their Spiritual and Mental Death that was caused by the Devil and his false teachings to the public. It is the spiritual poisoning of the population that takes time to remedy, and only truth can solve this Divine Problem. The Negroes are like a frozen embryo that needs the sunlight of Islam to thaw out, because their Minds are frozen.

MISUNDERSTANDING ABOUT THE BIBLE AND HOLY QURAN

The Bible and Holy Quran are spiritual books intended to lift up a people morally by giving instructions that pertains to God. The Bible is a religious book that has been revised and tampered with by King James (European). The Holy Quran is a Holy Book whose teachings have not been revised since it was revealed to Prophet Muhammad 1400 years ago. The correct understanding of these two books will open the eyes of the blind (Blackman) and make known to the world that what Master Fard Muhammad has revealed to the world is true.

The Whiteman is in control of Christianity and he has the public thinking that the Judgment takes place after a person dies. This is not True! The human spirit works in this manner. It becomes a chain by which man is bound by his good deeds or his evil deeds. The Rise and Fall of Man as foretold in the Bible and Holy Quran is due sorely to Man's inability or ability to live up to the Word of God. Nations, communities, and individuals are all constructed according to God's spiritual Laws in creation. The problem arise when people do not want to follow the guidelines of Scripture, and become lost, blind, deaf, and dumb to the ways of Self and God. The prescription of Love, Chastity, Fasting, Prayer, and being Thrifty is what God wants for the Righteous, but a mis-understanding of scripture can be disastrous to the human family.

GOG AND MAGOG

From a modern perspective, Gog and Magog refers to America and Russia or USA and USSR. Their overall identity is all European Nations that have spread across the planet and evolve into two distinct world powers, and these two powers control the planet today. The six-thousand years given to Gog and Magog to rule over Man by Mankind was up in 1914. Since that time, the world has been going through "A Changing Of The Guard" from the rule of Satan to the rule of God. The color of a person's skin has nothing to do with God's Righteousness during g this period of Spiritual Cleansing. Mankind is the one that makes a distinction between color and being right.

During this Grace Period given by God to Man so that he can clean himself up morally and spiritually is so that he can be made "Fit for the Kingdom of Heaven." If Man does not clean up, the judgment will set-in and Mankind and his lifestyle will be destroyed. The purpose of God coming to separate the Righteous from the Unrighteous, or the wheat from the tares is because Evil has had its day and ruled with a strong hand, now it is God's time to rule with Peace and Goodness. Black People in America have never had an opportunity to serve or worship their own God and practice their own Way of Life until now!

White people always denied black people this basic human right. There are many whites in America that fell they do not owe black people anything because he has been paid. Paid with what? A JOb, The opportunity to roam around America with poor housing, being beaten and lynched whenever caught outside our community? We have no banks, land to build houses, no hospitals or Schools to teach our children of their heritage. So I Ask, Blacks have been Paid What? Gog and Magog have not paid their debt to the Blackman and Woman of America, but God is going to see that Justice is done and the debt will be settled!

CAIN AND ABEL

There is another name that the Bible uses to identify White People and it is Cain. The name Cain represent White People and Abel represents Black People. The Bible uses symbolic names like Cain and Abel to indicate the characteristics of two people. Genesis 4:1-2 And Adam knew Eve his wife; and she conceived , and bare Cain, and said, I've gotten a Man from the Lord. And She again bare his brother Abel, and Abel was a keeper of sheep, but Cain was a tiller of the ground. And it came to pass that Cain brought an offer and Abel also made and offering to the Lord. The Lord had respect for the offering of Abel , but he did not have respect for Cain's offering.

God explained to Cain that if he does well, then his offering would be accepted. however, if he does not well, then his offering would not be accepted, if he does not well, it is because Sin lieth at the door. Cain was angry, and while in the field, Cain slew his brother Abel. And the Lord said unto Cain, Where is thy brother Abel, his blood crieth to me from the ground ? Cain said, I do not know, Am I My Brother's Keeper? God cursed Cain and said that henceforth he would be a vagabond and fugitive throughout the earth. Cain said that if this comes to pass then everyone that finds me will slay me , but God put a " mark" on Cain so that no one would kill him until God reveal who he was. The "mark" that God put on Cain was to Conceal his Identity as the Devil, A Born Killer to the human family of the earth! Cain would be safe to live on earth as long as God had his "Mark or Seal of Identity" on him.

Once God remove his mark then him time to live is up. God came in the person of Master Fard Muhammad and revealed that Cain was the White Race and their time was up to live and rule over Black Mankind. The Biblical account of Cain slew Abel is the European nations killing over six-hundred million blacks for every one thousand years that they have been on the earth. Cain left the presence of God and dwelt in the land of Nod, on the East of Eden (Europe).

JESUS AND THE RESURRECTION

Jesus spoke in parables , symbolism, and metaphors and one day his disciples said to him, why speakest thou in parables? (Matthew 13:10-11) He answered and said unto them, Because it is given unto you (Righteous) to know the mysteries of the Kingdom of Heaven, but to them (Unrighteous) it is not given. The mysteries that Jesus spoke about was the time of the end of this world of evil to rule over the righteous. Who were the spiritually dead people that had been killed by falsehood, lies, and misunderstanding about God. The dead would hear the truth and be resurrected from their graves and live. In the last days all the graves (nations) shall hear his voice (The second Jesus) and come forth to life or to damnation because of the evil that they had done.

JESUS AND NICHODEMUS

John 3:1-14 There was a man named Nicodemus, a ruler of the Jews. Nichodemus said unto him, how can a man be born when he is old? Can he enter the second time into his mother's womb, and be born? Jesus answered, verily, verily, I say unto thee, Except a man be born of water and of the spirit, he cannot enter the Kingdom of God. That which is born of flesh is flesh and that which is born of spirit is spirit. And Moses lifted up the serpent in the

153

wilderness, even so must the Son of Man be lifted up, that whosoever believeth in him should not perish but have eternal life.

The Blackman will be born again and receive eternal life by believing in this truth taught by the Son of Man (Fard Muhammad). The serpent (Europeans) that was lifted up in the wilderness (Europe) and put on the road to civilization by Moses was considered Born Again. White People was Born Again from the uncivilized life that they lived for over two-thousand years in the caves and hillsides of Europe. So it is that the wisdom of Allah will bring about a re-birth to the minds of the so-called Negroes in the Cave of America. The rebirth will be from a slave nation to a Muslim nation.

Mental and Spiritual separation is the key to the re-birth. The Negroes must be separated mentally so that they can be born-again in a new culture, religion, history, flag, economy and God. If black people do not accept this new birth then they will not be accepted by God, and are condemned to their own habits and behaviors placed in them by the Devil. Which is the final death, because in order to be born-again, they must be clean morally and spiritually to be the people of God.

JESUS WAS A SIGN OF THE LAST DAYS

There is more confusion over whether Jesus is alive or dead than any other man that has ever lived. Why? Jesus of two-thousand years ago was a sign of something to come. He was born out of wedlock and had to be hidden from the public's eye, for his own protection, until he

154

matured because he was destined to teach the Jews to return to the Laws of Moses. He failed in his mission.

Two-thousand years later, the Blackman (So-Called Negroes) are born out of wedlock from their own nation, and have been hidden from the world for over 400 years, because they are destined to fulfill Jesus mission of teaching the world righteousness, in these Last Days of Satan's Rule. They will be successful! What purpose would it serve to have Jesus die, hide from the public for two thousand years, and then brought back to life to complete his mission of converting white people. THIS DOES NOT MAKE SENSE, the Blackman of America will complete the mission of Jesus by bringing the world back to Righteousnes

The correct interpretation of scripture is vital to the re-birth of the Blackman and woman of America because the Bible is as poisonous to their Minds as a rattlesnake if it is not understood. The truth that this book gives will clear up some of the misunderstandings about Jesus, White People, Black People, God and the Devil.

All prophets have been called liars, and been rejected in the King James Version because it was revised by a White man named King James, just as Emperor Augustus Constantine revised Christianity at the Council of Nicea. However, the Holy Quran has not been revised and edited; Read it and learn all about yourself!

CONCLUSION

THE BLACKMAN'S MIND MUST BE RE-MADE INTHE IMAGE OF A GODLY AFROCENTRIC MIND!

Matthew 21: 42-44 Jesus said to them, did ye ever read in the scriptures, The stone that the builders rejected, the same has become the head of the corner; this is the Lord's doing, and it is marvelous in our eyes? Therefore I say unto you, The Kingdom of God shall be taken from you, and given to a nation bringing forth the fruits of it. And whosoever shall fall on this stone shall be grind to powder.

The stone in this parable of Jesus is the so-called Negroes whom (God) will make into a great nation with power, and under his Divine Guidance. Anyone trying to destroy this work is playing with fire, and will be ground into powder. The stone that has been rejected by the whole world as a nation is the So Called Negroes of America, and the builders is the leading nations of earth. Allah will bring them low as he build the Negroes into a foundation of Righteousness over other nations. This is known scriptural as Raising Dead Nations to life, Holy Quran Ch 6, Section 15, Verse 817 states that not only were the dead raised to life, but they now had a "Light" within them to show others the way to God.

Although despised and rejected by the world-community, God has chosen the Negroes as his people. God's light is the greatest light of all in this world of darkness. But to have his light reflected in your being, one

156

must practice his ways and behavior. The light that God brings to the Negroes is Islam, and the book is the Holy Quran, and the interpretation is from God (Master Fard Muhammad) and not from some scholars in the Devil's World. No nation has been more spiritually Blind, Deaf. and Dumb than the Blackman of America. When they wake up, and they will, it will fulfill the scripture in Genesis 15:13 that after 400 years, God will come and bring them out with great sustenance. The stone that the Builders (world leaders) rejected will be taken from the European Nations and bring forth the fruits of Righteousness that God has intended for his people. All the Black nations that are captured mentally, and physically by White nations are in Hell. They are suffering from wars, starvation, and a lack of governmental control within their own nations.

The European nations are in Heaven on earth because they are in control of the fish, land, sky, and other nations on earth. The Whiteman' s heaven is a Blackman's hell. However, the Europeans have been unable to bring about salvation to the people (Righteous living according to Divine Laws). They have destroyed most of the earth since they have been the overseer. They love deviant behavior in sex, lying, stealing money, fornication, and generally a law-breaker. The people selected by God to become the Head of the Black Nations to rule the world will be the so-called Negroes because they have suffered the most with lost of heritage, history, name, culture, economy, and slavery.

Re-made in God's Image

This idea may seem impossible to you, but it was the same in Pharaoh's days when he laughed at the very thought of the Children of Israel having a government of their own and ruling themselves because he knew that he had not taught them how to govern self, and they had no economy, land , connections with other governments, or most of all they Loved Their Slavemaster and Did Not Want To Be Separate.

So in reality, it looks like a case of futility trying to raise the Negroes (Children of Isreal) out of the Hell in this government to the heavenly condition of having your own government, but all things are possible with God. Allah has said that the negroes will become the cornerstone of the new world. A nation that has been raised as slaves within another nation cannot ever achieve equality with the master. No master has ever shared his wealth equally with his slaves the slave must earn his own freedom and then establish his own self-sufficiency. The So Called Negroes think that they are equal by-law with the Whiteman of America but it is not true. The Whiteman has an unwritten Law that no Black Person will ever become the head of this government because it would signal an end to his rule.

The Blackman is fooled through politics that he can become the head or President of the United States, this is done to keep his pacified to live under white rule, which in six thousand years have killed six hundred million black people around the world. The Blackman and woman must have a New Government of Righteousness "ISLAM". The mental and spiritual bondage with the devil must be broken.

Why is the Blackman and woman of America referred to as Negroes and other blacks referred to as Jamaican, Nigerian, Haitian, or Ethiopian. It is because all the other black nations still have their Nationality, Culture, History, Flag, and Religion. Whereas the Negroes have been stripped of their Nationality and are homeless in America within the framework of the American Government. A Whiteman Heaven (Government) is a Blackman's Hell. THE MOST VITAL ESSENTIAL TO BUILDING A GOVERNMENT IS YOUR HISTORY, CULTURE AND RELIGION; This government will not even acknowledge that they robbed us of these essential pearls of spiritual life, or that THEY NAMED THE BLACKMAN A NEGRO AS A SYMBOL THAT HE WAS MENTALLY DEAD.

This spiritual condition of being dead to Who You Are and in love with your enemy has caused the Negroes to be despised and rejected by others black nations, because they have the whiteman's name, culture and identity in this modern day of education. The other black nations know that they cannot trust the Negroes as brothers until they change their philosophy , names, and start to think as a Blackman. Even so, God has chosen to re-make the Mind of the Blackman to be a superior thinker and teach the other nations that which they did not, and still do not know about the Whiteman, the times, and the future.

Believe it or Not, the Blackman and Woman of America are fulfilling Scripture and Prophecy, they are Divine people and if one were to study their character and natural tendencies instead of the habits acquired in this society, it is easy to see that they are the people of God. This is a transitional period of time for a change in world-powers. Since this book is about how the Blackman was made a Negro by the Whiteman , and not by natural creation of God, let us study the term "Colored" as a psychological tool in slave-making.

The Whiteman states that the Blackman is a Colored Man but this is not true because the Blackman is the father or originator of Color for all the races. The originator cannot be equal to that which he makes, the name for the originator is simply "Original". From Black comes colors or that which is color-ed. The term color-ed means past tensed or that which comes from an original color. The colors that comes from Black are the Japanese (Brown), Red (Indians), Chinese (Yellow), and Caucasian (White). These races are your color-ed people on earth and should be referred to as the colored people of earth. There is a lesson in Islam that state it this way.

Who Is the Original Man? Who Is The Colored Man? The Original Man is the Blackman, Maker, Owner, Cream of the Planet earth, God of the Universe. The Colored Man is the Whiteman, Yacub's grafted devil, the skunk of the planet earth. Everything of God has been turned around to make it appear that the Blackman is the lesser of the two people but this is not true. Let us look at the Food. God has forbidden the touching of the swine, but what is the main staple of this government and the tables of the negrpes---Pig! The swine is a grafted animal between the Cat, Rat and the Dog, He has the dog's body, the cat's ears, and the rat's tail. He has 999 germs in his body and a sewage line between his split hoof , that runs pus continuously, and if plugged up it would kill him instantly. He is so poisonous that he can eat poison (eat snakes and get fat) it will not harm him. He is ugly, greedy, shyless, and careless, Once a person begin to eat this creature, they lose shyness and a portion of their beauty appearance. One of the first things that God intend to change when the Blackman is in his own government is his dietary law.

Now, we know that the Blackman is not a Negro or Colored Man, nor Afro American because that is only a transitional term and not his nature. The next government will be based on the nature of the Blackman which is Muslim or One Who Submits entirely to the Will Of God. The term Islam describes all the fundamental principles of being a Muslim, Holy Quran, and general guidelines. This is a New Islam patterned after the teachings of Hon. Elijah Muhammad and Fard Muhammad not Orthodox Islam patterned after the Arabs of 1400 years ago. There will be new concepts of Man and the Woman, New ideas of how to eat, new understanding about heaven and hell, new perspective on re-incarnation, and a totally new understanding of God and the Devil.

Orthodox Islam cannot provide the Blackman of America (Negroes) with the power and strength to break the mental and spiritual chains that bound his Mind, but Islam as taught by the Hon. Elijah Muhammad will do just that. A modern-day Muslim is a Mind of Righteousness.

161

A Mind of Progress and a Mind Made by God and Not the Whiteman. The Blackman must have his own religion (Islam), the Whiteman has Christianity, the Jews have Judaism, and the Japanese and Chinese have Buddhism. Islam changes the Consciousness of the Negro to see himself as he really is, he never was a Negro, that was thrust upon the Blackman in slavery and it is still a burden to his growth and development.

Always remember, that Black and White People are "TWO DIFFERENT PEOPLE WITH TWO DIFFERENT NATURES" and this is why the two can never lived together in harmony and peace. It is like a cat and dog being raised up in the same house, they may co-exist because of the owner but by nature they are not to live together in the same house, there will always be confusion. Holy Quran Chapter 15, Section 3, verses 26-40 explains the creation of the Blackman and the Whiteman, and the opposition that the Whiteman has in bowing down or submitting to the Blackman, his maker.

Allah states that there are two creation operating on earth at the same time (This is in every phase of life ; two types of fish in competition, two types of animals in competition , in every phase of life including human life). The two human creations in competition is the Black and White i.e. brown, red, yellow are considered a part of the black family. The Blackman was created first from sounding clay, of black mud fashioned into shape. From the blackman, Allah created the Races, and the last color is White, and he was created of intensely hot fire, and became the opposite of the sounding clay (Blackman). The sounding clay of black mud fashioned into shape and intensely hot fire, shows the characteristics and temperaments of these two creations. The Blackman is of the earth and was fashioned spiritually by Allah, by breathing into him the Divine Spirit, thus giving him perfection , from dust to perfection, the way of all Divine Growth from God.

White people created with a fiery nature or temperament tends to lead self and others away from Gods Laws and are rebellious. Whatever God says "Thou Shall Not Do" they say "We Will Do" There nature is to rebel against Divine Law and that is why the scripture writers say that they were made for fuel for the Fire from the beginning of their creation. The Blackman's creation from dust to perfection shows a humbleness to Divine Law and a submission to God and his way of life.

Throughout this book, Sixty Four Years To Make A Negro, I have attempted to show you that the Whiteman has a history of destroying black people. From Adam and Eve being driven out of the Garden to the caves and hill-sides of Europe where they spent two-thousand years living as animals and eating bugs out of the ground. To Cain and Abel Genesis 4:14 wherein Cain killed his brother Abel (Blackman) and was made a vagabond and fugitive until God would come and reveal who he was to the rest of the human family; at the end of time God revealed that the Whiteman is the cause of the world's problems.

The end of time was the end of Satan's time to rule the earth (White People). The Blackman has been made a Negro (Dead Man) in America, and God is fulfilling scripture by raising this dead man back to life, after this the Judgment will set in, and punishment will begin because nations will rise up against the injustice causing world-wide tragedy. The Devil will not go down easy, he said that he would make everyone of earth turn against God and his laws (Job) and would make evil appear to be normal or fair-seeming. He would caused them all to fall from Grace, except the purified ones (righteous Muslims) that are raised during the Resurrection or Judgment.

Allah said to Satan (White People) all of those who follow you, I will fill hell up with them all. Hell has seven gates or many ways , and hell is for a portion or remedial time because God comes to save the righteous and destroy the wicked. The Negro cannot build the Kingdom of Heaven because his mind is not of God but of the Devil. He must have a new Mind of a Muslim to be able to build this new world of God.

Fro a Negro to A Muslim is a great educational experience, but the Devil must pay for what he has done to our people, this is God's business. But Remember this WARNING----YOU MUST WANT TO BE SAVED IN ORDER TO BE SAVED, BELIEF ALONE COUNTS FOR NOTHING, YOU MUST ACTIVELY SEEK SALVATION! hurry, and Join on to your own nation, the Nation of Islam, and follow the teachings of God , Master Fard Muhammad and his servant Hon. Elijah Muhammad.

Throughout this book there is one continuous principle ---The Image Of The Mind Is What Makes A Man What He Is! The Blackman gave the Image of government and civilization to the Whiteman. The Whiteman forced the Image of being a Negro into the Mind of the Blackman. Now, God has come to re-educate and re-build the Mind of the Blackman into his own Image. Remember, YOU ARE WHAT YOU THINK, AN IMAGE IS THE PRODUCT OF THOUGHT, and the Negro is the product of the thinking of the Whiteman and not a creation of God. The Blackman and Woman is God's creation.

"MILLION MAN MARCH"

THE MILLION MAN MARCH IS A DAY OF ATONEMENT FOR THE BLACK NATION IN AMERICA AND A FULFILLMENT OF SCRIPTURE. Lev.23:28 And ye shall do no work in that day; for it is a day of atonement (Reconciliation),to make an atonemnet for you before the Lord your God. Remember that the stone (Black people) that the builders (America) rejected will become the cornerstone of the whole nation. Thank You Min. Farrakhan, Rev. Chavis and the Black Leadership.

Peace Be Unto You!

NOTES

NOTES

NOTES

NOTES

NOTES